D0194110

"A distinctive anthology of Asian American vo.
gender, sexism and racism within the context of an overarching Christian faith."
CLAIRE S. CHOW, AUTHOR OF *LEAVING DEEP WATER: THE LIVES OF ASIAN-AMERICAN WOMEN AT THE CROSSROADS OF TWO CULTURES*

"Boldly exposes the key struggles Asian American Christian women face in embracing their personal identity in Christ and expressing their kingdom discipleship interacting with critical issues like ethnicity, gender, family, society, traditions, etc. With a brimful of insights and inspiration, this volume is a must-read for both genders of all races and cultures."
DR. T. V. THOMAS, COCHAIR, INTERNATIONAL NETWORK OF SOUTH ASIAN DIASPORA LEADERS (INSADL)

"Finally, a work that recognizes the hard work and devotion of a 'sometimes' overlooked part of God's kingdom: Asian American women in his service. May the testimonies represented in the stories of challenge and joy from five women, their spheres of influence, be used one hundred times to bless those who have faithfully served, but even more that they would encourage those just beginning journeys of faithfulness. A must-read for all (especially mothers, sisters, 'aunties' and the brothers) who come alongside women who fully desire to serve God and his people in their giftedness and excellence for his glory."
REV. MELANIE MAR CHOW, ASIAN AMERICAN CHRISTIAN FELLOWSHIP, CAMPUS MINISTER, JEMS/AACF

"*More Than Serving Tea* is a testimony of how God has made us—including our ethnic and gender identities—fearfully and wonderfully. I especially appreciate how the authors highlight the specific strengths of Asian American Christian women. By weaving together personal narrative with biblical insights, their stories capture how God can redeem and use our emerging Asian American culture to serve his kingdom."
RUSSELL JEUNG, ASSOCIATE PROFESSOR OF ASIAN AMERICAN STUDIES, SAN FRANCISCO STATE UNIVERSITY, AND AUTHOR OF *FAITHFUL GENERATIONS: RACE AND NEW ASIAN AMERICAN CHURCHES*

"*More Than Serving Tea* is an insightful and moving collection of essays by Asian American Christian women. This book is a valuable resource for anyone wanting to understand their unique experiences and an inspiration for those who face similar challenges."
MICHELLE V. LEE, PH.D., ASSISTANT PROFESSOR OF BIBLICAL STUDIES AND THEOLOGY, BIOLA UNIVERSITY

"*More Than Serving Tea* is a timely contribution and gift to the Asian American community. It affirms the unique contributions that Asian American women bring to our diverse cultural landscape as well as challenges our culture to break the stereotypes that many of us still cling to. This book also serves as a personal reminder of the gifts that our mothers, sisters, wives and daughters bring to us. Through this work, the authors provide worthy spiritual role models and mentors with whom I would entrust my own daughter."

SOONG-CHAN RAH, MILTON B. ENGEBRETSON ASSISTANT PROFESSOR OF EVANGELISM AND CHURCH GROWTH, NORTH PARK THEOLOGICAL SEMINARY, CHICAGO, ILLINOIS

"I wish this book had been around ten to fifteen years ago! But thankfully, it is here now. I was blessed by the honest stories and thoughtful reflections from this group of accomplished Asian American Christian leaders. *More Than Serving Tea* is more than just a good read. Asian American readers of all ages will learn from the collective wisdom and experiences within."

HELEN LEE, FORMER ASSISTANT EDITOR OF *CHRISTIANITY TODAY*, COFOUNDER OF THE BEST CHRISTIAN WORKPLACES INSTITUTE, AND COEDITOR OF *GROWING HEALTHY ASIAN AMERICAN CHURCHES*

"*More Than Serving Tea* unveils the Western 'mystique' about Asian American women and shows us what an emerging generation of Asian American Christian women leaders are thinking. The richly textured voices of U.S.-born or raised Asian American women—often silenced in their families and churches—are wonderfully woven into a tapestry of honest stories of pain, struggle, joy and Christian hope. One does not need to be a woman or an Asian American to learn something about faith, discipleship and Asian American Christianity from this landmark book!"

DR. TIM TSENG, PRESIDENT, INSTITUTE FOR THE STUDY OF ASIAN AMERICAN CHRISTIANITY

"*More Than Serving Tea* is a passionate anthology of personal stories that will enlighten Asian women and provide a rich perspective to anyone who works with this rapidly growing ethnic group. It will challenge Asian women to impact their communities by being authentic to their true calling in life. May this critical resource inspire you to 'live out loud' and reach your full potential as well!"

JANE HYUN, EXECUTIVE COACH/DIVERSITY STRATEGIST, AND AUTHOR OF *BREAKING THE BAMBOO CEILING: CAREER STRATEGIES FOR ASIANS*

"*More Than Serving Tea* is an exciting and inspiring collection of *becoming* of Asian American women as they negotiate their faith at the intersection of race, gender, class, sexuality and spirituality. As faithful practitioners of their faith, each author is a witness to the strength of her character, the depth and width of her desire to better understand how faith is lived out in the complex web of relationships that comprise our everyday living. Their stories are hauntingly familiar while the strength and courage of their hope is impressively palpable. The sheer honesty present throughout this book makes this a must-read for women in search of what it means to be strong, Christian and Asian American in North America!"

ANNE JOH, ASSISTANT PROFESSOR OF THEOLOGY, PHILLIPS THEOLOGICAL SEMINARY, AND AUTHOR OF *HEART OF THE CROSS: A POSTCOLONIAL CHRISTOLOGY*

"Here is the world of Asian American women, unadorned. Diverse and immediate, these stories unveil a culture marked by shame, self-doubt, silence, invalidation, misogyny and great harm. Yet Jesus' strong call sounds in the midst: 'Name what is unjust, right what is wrong, love deeply in the midst of pain, and become the strong message bearers of the gospel you were created to be.' A book of clarity and courage."

SALLY MORGENTHALER, AUTHOR OF *WORSHIP EVANGELISM*, AND FOUNDER, CONVERSATIONS: GATHERINGS FOR WOMEN OF SUBSTANCE, WWW.TRUECONVERSATIONS.COM

"What a gift this book is to the community of Christian women. Filled with solid biblical wisdom and slumber-party transparency, *More Than Serving Tea* made me feel like I was surrounded by a team of women who were walking me down a path toward Jesus. As a Caucasian woman, I found this book particularly helpful. Not only am I better able to understand and encourage the Asian American women in my life, but I also found myself challenged personally with my own shortcomings of people-pleasing, perfectionism, suffering, relationships and leadership. *More Than Serving Tea* is a must-read for all young Christian women who are hungry for a deeper walk with God and some companions to help you journey."

MICHELLE GRAHAM, AUTHOR OF *WANTING TO BE HER: BODY IMAGE SECRETS VICTORIA WON'T TELL YOU*

"A fascinating book that brings to light the struggles, hardships, joys and blessings that many Asian American women experience as they live in this foreign land. The honesty and openness of these stories intricately connect to biblical images and are simply good for the soul. Toyama and Gee have edited an indispensable and delightful collection of essays for the Asian American community and the wider North American community as we live in a multicultural and globalized world."

GRACE JI-SUN KIM, AUTHOR OF *THE GRACE OF SOPHIA*, AND ASSISTANT PROFESSOR OF DOCTRINAL THEOLOGY, MORAVIAN THEOLOGICAL SEMINARY

"*More Than Serving Tea* is a collection of rare, intimate, lived stories of Asian American women Christians. These stories are rare because they include struggles against Asian patriarchalism, American racism and interethnic stereotypes. Particularly, the review of mainstream film's portrayal of the Asian American female grabs the reader's attention powerfully. The power of image, language and symbols in motion pictures defines Asian American women's location within the American society. Nevertheless, in this book the silent, submissive, exotic speaks and challenges the superimposed script from the motion pictures, family and the church. By telling our own stories, we shape Asian American Christian women's identity according to God's design."

REV. YOUNG LEE HERTIG, PH.D., GLOBAL STUDIES AND SOCIOLOGY DEPARTMENT, AZUSA PACIFIC UNIVERSITY

"God, in his wisdom and creativity, has created each of us in a unique way. Some he designed to be Asian American Christian women, a specific grouping that is not often addressed in Asian American literature. This book is an honest look at the personal struggles that these women deal with and how God corrects, heals and empowers them so that they can more fully embrace the whole package of who God made them."

JIMMY LEE, EXECUTIVE DIRECTOR, THE WHITE HOUSE INITIATIVE ON ASIAN AMERICANS AND PACIFIC ISLANDERS

Nikki A. Toyama and Tracey Gee, EDITORS,

Kathy Khang, Christie Heller de Leon and Asifa Dean

CONSULTING EDITOR, Jeanette Yep

More Than Serving Tea

ASIAN AMERICAN WOMEN ON

EXPECTATIONS, RELATIONSHIPS,

LEADERSHIP AND FAITH

IVP Books

An imprint of InterVarsity Press
Downers Grove, Illinois

InterVarsity Press
P.O. Box 1400, Downers Grove, IL 60515-1426
World Wide Web: www.ivpress.com
E-mail: email@ivpress.com

InterVarsity Press® is the book-publishing division of InterVarsity Christian Fellowship/USA®, a student movement active on campus at hundreds of universities, colleges and schools of nursing in the United States of America, and a member movement of the International Fellowship of Evangelical Students. For information about local and regional activities, write Public Relations Dept., InterVarsity Christian Fellowship/USA, 6400 Schroeder Rd., P.O. Box 7895, Madison, WI 53707-7895, or visit the IVCF website at <www.intervarsity.org>.

Scripture quotations, unless otherwise noted, are from the New Revised Standard Version of the Bible, copyright 1989 by the Division of Christian Education of the National Council of the Churches of Christ in the USA. Used by permission. All rights reserved.

While all of the stories in this book are true, some names and identifying details have been altered to protect the privacy of those involved.

Design: Cindy Kiple

Images: border: Emilia Kun/istockphoto.com
        background: istockphoto.com
        Chinese blossom: Susi Bikle/istockphoto.com

ISBN-10: 0-8308-3371-4
ISBN-13: 978-0-8308-3371-9

Printed in the United States of America ∞

Library Of Congress Cataloging-in-Publication Data

More than serving tea/edited by Nikki A. Toyama and Tracey Gee.
    p. cm.
    Includes bibliographical references.
    ISBN-13: 978-0-8308-3371-9 (pbk.: alk. paper)
    ISBN-10: 0-8308-3371-4 (pbk.: alk. paper)
    1. Asian American women—Religious life. 2. Women—Religious
aspects—Christianity. I. Toyama, Nikki A., 1974- 11. Gee, Tracey,
1974-
BR563.A82M67 2006
277.3'083082—dc22

                                                                    2006030079

P	19	18	17	16	15	14	13	12	11	10	9	8	7	6	5
Y	21	20	19	18	17	16	15	14	13	12	11	10	09			

To our mothers, sisters,

and those who guided us along the way.

Contents

Foreword

*A*nother wedding banquet. Another food fest. Twelve family members and relatives crowded around a table. Some gossiping and catching up. One or two reading a book. All of us greedily eating appetizers and waiting for the arrival of the bride and groom so we can "officially" begin the food orgy.

During the long wait for the guests of honor, relatives and friends come by the table to greet us: "My, how you have grown!" "How is school? Work?" Then the *real* question, "When are you going to get married so I can come to *your* wedding banquet?" With their eyes on the prize, my well-meaning Chinese relatives wanted me to reach the big goal of life—marriage, husband, children and grandchildren. Unfortunately, I've not run the race according to the ancient rules.

Long, long ago in a land far away, a script for being female in a patriarchal culture was written. Generations later, in a new land, the script is not easily changed. Fashion, language, religious, economic and educational circumstances may be different, but role and gender expectations seem to change at a glacial pace.

Being Asian, American and female—and a follower of Jesus as well—makes growing up hard to do! Is there a way of doing all of it well?

In this book, five wonderful young women, who have this same struggle, talk about their lives, their families, their challenges, their joys. They all grew up biculturally in the United States, but they represent East Asian (Japanese [Nikki], Korean [Kathy] and Chinese [Tracey]) cultures and the new voices of the South Asian (Pakistani [Asifa]) and Southeast Asian (Filipina [Christie]) experience. As we have spent time together and learned from one another in a leadership development and mentoring program sponsored by InterVarsity Christian Fellowship, I have come to appreciate each of these women in a unique way. I am honored to know them!

The authors investigate the intersection of gender, race and Christian discipleship by addressing questions related to parents, expectations, suffering, perfectionism, friendship, sexuality, stereotypes, leadership and finding one's voice. Simple answers don't show up in these chapters. But integrity and authenticity are here, making the book ring true.

Asian American women (and those who love them) will find this book speaking to them in specific ways. But in addition, readers from any culture will find great help in these stories and insights. As you consider the freedom God wants his children to have, may you grow far beyond merely serving tea. Jesus offers wholeness that benefits the entire family of God. Read on and see how.

Jeanette Yep
Harare, Zimbabwe

Introduction

ASIAN AMERICAN CHRISTIAN WOMEN:
Triple Blessing or Triple Curse?

NIKKI A. TOYAMA

I arrived in Thailand, the third leg of my trip. I had visited the urban slums of Cairo and Nairobi, and now I was in Bangkok. I was working on a project looking at the vulnerability of women among the urban poor. My project brought me to the red-light district of Bangkok.

I immediately felt at home in Thailand. The support railings in the trains stood at the perfect height for me to reach. I blended in with the crowd and fit in the local clothes sizes, and the food was amazing.

One day, while waiting for a friend, I sat on the steps outside a mall. Looking around, I noticed signs in Japanese and discreet entrances—the Japanese red-light district. This area catered to Japanese businessmen. We had been working, a few streets over, in the American red-light district. There Thai women catered to an American clientele. With my eyes now open, I began to notice other districts for German, British, French clients. Thai women were made available to all these men. I had no idea there was a district for each group. The streets extended for blocks—row after row of brothels and bars.

That night, I went back to the Japanese red-light district. I walked and asked God, "What do you want me to see?" I prayed for the women who worked in that area and for the men who were their patrons. I prayed for the wives and daughters of the men coming to these bars. I prayed against the broken systems in our society that promote and provide space for these industries. As I watched women call men into the bars, I prayed. After a couple of hours, I went home.

As I rode home on the train, I wondered what it meant for me, a Japanese American Christian. A Caucasian man approached me to ask a question. Before speaking, he looked over my body, from my legs to my face, though I was wearing very conservative missionary clothes. He was shameless. He did not try to mask his appraisal: he looked over my body as if assessing a product. I recognized this look—I had seen it repeatedly in the red-light district as the men entered the bars.

I had never felt so violated. The country marketed its sex industry too well, and I, though an outsider, felt its burden. Behaviors like freely staring at women's bodies were tolerated and promoted even. In that place, as an Asian woman, I was told, in effect, that my only contribution was as a sexual object.

I ran home from the train that night. I went to the room I shared with six others. Thankful that it was empty, I sat on my bed, a mat in the only air-conditioned corner of a slum church, and cried. I cried for myself, but then I cried for the women of Thailand.

I had visited urban slums in two other countries, Kenya and Egypt. Even though both places were significantly poorer (the monthly income in Nairobi was $30, Cairo $60, Bangkok $120), very few parents there would sell their little daughters into prostitution as parents do in Thailand. What makes a country and its families treat its women with so little regard? I thought of the women I met in the Kibera slum in Nairobi—as poor as they were, they would never sell their children.

Misogyny runs deep in Asia. Families abandon little baby girls in the Chinese countryside, waiting for a son. In Japan, college-educated girls are openly discriminated against in the workplace—they are passed over for promotions because it is assumed they will leave the workplace once they marry. The sex trade in Asia continues to enslave women; Taiwan has the highest per capita prostitution rate, while Japan has criminal syndicates kidnapping and trafficking women all over Asia. Thailand was the capital of sex trafficking until Cambodia gained that dubious distinction. *Why does Asia hate its women?*

Just as I was getting ready to shake my fist at God in anger, he reminded me that he weeps more for these women than I do. God weeps for these women, who are made in his image. He looks at each of them and sees a precious daughter. Where others see a prostitute, he sees his child. He wants to speak words of dignity and tell her that she's beloved. Others say "worthless," "useless," "less than," but he speaks the word *chosen*. She is chosen by him to steward the gift of being a woman and an Asian.

Jesus knows personally the pain of being judged, misunderstood, underestimated. He knows what it means to be shunned by others and have your body bought and sold. He knows the depth of the sorrow and the pain of the women in the red-light district of Bangkok. I could catch only a glimpse.

That night, as I prayed for the women, I found myself blaming their ethnicity and their gender for their situations. The prostitution that I witnessed, the lack of options for Asian women,

> *My identity as an Asian American and my identity as a woman are just beginning to merge within me as a singular identity, and I am feeling a missionary zeal to let others know about it.*
>
> MITSUYE YAMADA

the attitudes of the community did not connect with what I thought was God's truth. Are they made in his image? Are they precious and chosen? Does God care about their situation? That night, God began to show me that he did not make a mistake—one ethnicity or gender is not better than another. He had chosen to make each of those women Thai and female. And in the same way, I was not a mistake. God chose to make me Japanese and female. The process of embracing my gender and my ethnicity began that night.

I had spent most of my academic life trying to overcome the perceived flaws of my gender and of my race. In class I would speak first and speak often. I played sports during free time—basketball, football, ultimate. I didn't want to be some Asian girl who was scared of being dirty. I loved the look of surprise from the guys on the field when they asked, "Do you play?"

Over the years I began to see how some "flaws" of my gender and race became God's tools for redemption. I hated my grandparents' refusal to tell me stories of what it was like to be Japanese American during World War II. But God returned that back to me as the gift of long-suffering. I hated the way my friends clumped together at social gatherings, so I asserted my independence. But God returned it to me as the gift of interdependence. I despised my programmed politeness that kept me from saying the angry words that boiled up within me. But God returned that to me as graciousness.

God reassured me that of all the ethnicities and genders he could have chosen for me, he chose Asian and female. He took my flaws and redeemed them to be used for his kingdom. My gender and ethnicity are God's gift to me—not an obstacle to overcome. These are my gifts to steward for others and for his kingdom.

MORE THAN SERVING TEA

Asian Pacific Islander women live in tension. We live between "Asian" and "American," "woman" and "daughter." Society has strong scripts for people of different ethnicities. And within those scripts, Asian culture has expectations and socially appropriate roles. Navigating multiple worlds is an everyday reality for the authors of this book. Kathy was a successful journalist who became a powerful manager in a nonprofit organization. But when she returns home, her father-in-law expects her to cut him fruit and make him a sandwich. I go from being a conference speaker one moment to being mistaken for a college freshman the next. We may be women of impressive accomplishments, but we are regularly called "cute" and mistaken for teens because of our size.

The roads to being a woman, being Asian, being American, being a Christian are each paved and well marked. But when they are combined, which road do we choose? Asian Pacific Islander women and our situations are as diverse as the many glorious body types that we come in. We want to share our stories of the ways that we've navigated the journey. We want to share our experiences, our struggles, our discoveries, in the hope of helping more women discover the truth about who God made them to be and how that can be used to accomplish his purposes.

Serving tea or chai is the women's role in many Asian Pacific Islander family circles. Often, young girls are taught the rituals. Stir the pot this way, hold your wrist just so, serve the most important guest first. The rituals pass down, from mother to daughter, secrets of the kitchen. Serving tea is a stereotype, but it also embodies great features of Asian culture—hospitality and service. Serving tea may be a simple act, but sometimes we are serving more than tea. At times, this cultural act is serving comfort, care or compassion to friends or family.

But Asian women are not limited to serving tea and sympathy. In this day of grande Tazo tea from Starbucks (two bags, please), women do more than serve tea. We serve our communities, our companies, our churches and our God. We want to embrace the positive attributes of Asian traditions and celebrate the gifts that culture brings to God's kingdom while letting go of the stereotypes that limit women to that role.

Each culture has unique gifts that help us to know God. From the Jews we learn about Jesus the Messiah, a sacrificial Lamb slain for the forgiveness of sins. From the Greeks we learn about God as the God of heaven and earth, the Maker of all things. From black American culture we learn about a God who loves justice. From Latino culture we learn about God's *familia*. Does our Asian culture have a gift that reflects a unique aspect of God? Specifically, is there something in being an Asian American woman that God has given us to share with the wider family?

Each of the writers in this book shares from her interactions mentoring a variety of young Asian, Asian American and Pacific Islander women around the country. We are from the East Coast, West Coast and Midwest. We hope and dream that women will discover that their gender and their ethnicity are God's gift to them. We want to share our stories and our journeys to help others navigate the paths linking family, culture, community, society and God.

This book stretches the boundaries past the place where typical "Asian" books leave off. Many Asian American books refer just to East Asia—Korea,

China, Taiwan, Japan. This book includes the voices of our sisters from South Asia (Pakistan, India) and Southeast Asia (Philippines, Cambodia, Thailand). As authors, we also tried to represent the voices of our biracial sisters; in addition, we tried to include the stories of women who grew up in different environments—adopted, raised in Asian communities, raised in non-Asian communities. Many other categories differentiate and pull us together—Islander versus mainland, immigration generation. One challenge was speaking from a Pakistani Christian perspective, fully aware of the Muslim tension. Throughout the book, different authors use "Asian American" or "Asian Pacific Islander." Each term works well for different communities, so each writer uses her own words.

This book was written for Asian Pacific Islander women and for the people who care for them. The process of giving voice to these experiences, a process of tears, fears, late nights and too much caffeine, was also a redemptive journey for us, our families and our communities. May the same be true for you.

Box
pulled
Asian   American

I check "other"
again

1

Sticks, Stones and Stereotypes

CHRISTIE HELLER DE LEON

Suzie Wong. Flower Drum Song. Dragon Lady. Madame Butterfly. China Doll.

Tokyo Rose . . . Savage. Mysterious. Inscrutable. Sinister. Exotic. Submissive.

Diminutive. Indolent. Insolent. Sexless. Sexy. Mail Order Bride. Model Minority.

I could go on and on, listing familiar and not so familiar stereotypes, drawing

from the abundant arsenal of dehumanizing images that assault us daily in America,

as we sleep and dream, as we eat, work, and study. What is this ghastly sickness all about?

The heart of darkness?

JESSICA HAGEDORN IN *ASIAN AMERICAN DREAMS*

Breakfast at Tiffany's, South Pacific, Elvis Presley's *Blue Hawaii.* My father loved to watch these movies as he grew up in the Philippines. They pictured the amazing lives of Americans falling in and out of love, fighting the enemy in wars, yet always able to dance or sing. My father continued to enjoy these movies in adulthood because they took him back to his youth. They reminded him of air-conditioned movie theaters, the music he enjoyed listening to and his dreams of coming to America.

As a kid growing up in America, I, too, watched these films. In fact, I really enjoyed them. Everyone on the television screen was eye candy. The men were strong, handsome and blue-eyed. Many of the women, especially in the films about Asia or the Pacific islands, were olive skinned with toned bodies and long black hair. These women seemed ready to shake their hips at the drop of a hat.

But one character was different: Mickey Rooney in *Breakfast at Tiffany's*. He played the awkward Japanese upstairs neighbor to Audrey Hepburn's Holly Golightly. He was far from beautiful. As a child I did not understand why a white man was playing a Japanese man. I learned later that Yellow-face was Hollywood's racist representation of people like me—buck teeth, taped-back eyelids and purposefully broken English. These were the "Asians" in the U.S. media of the 1950s and 1960s.

In my own youth, the voice of Long Duk Dong of *Sixteen Candles* rang in my ears. He was a socially and sexually awkward exchange student who, like Rooney, spoke in broken English. I laughed along with my friends as they imitated his accent.

But I felt a pit in my stomach watching Mickey Rooney or mimicking Long Duk Dong. As a teenager, I could not put my finger on the uneasy feeling I had. Maybe I knew that I was breaking the "kindergarten" rules of not making fun of people. Maybe I felt sorry for those characters. Or maybe I wanted to separate myself from those odd people on television. What I realize now is that I felt both in awe and ashamed of the two men. I was in awe that people who *supposedly* looked like me made it into the movies. Yet I was ashamed that they seemed freakishly awkward.

As Asian American women today, we face stereotypes that attempt to define and limit who we are. Politics, media and our own American culture attempt to tell us who we are and what our potential is. However, God's desire is for us to know deeply the inherent worth, value and honor he gives us. God wants to take the destructive names given to us and rename us in his loving terms. And on those terms, he empowers us to be leaders in the marketplace and the church.

TRUTH BE TOLD

A stereotype is an oversimplification of a concept or image. A sexual stereotype bases the oversimplification on sexual characteristics. Although sexuality is a God-given gift, sexual stereotypes distort the gift, making people one-dimensional and objectified. Historically, women in general have suffered from the stereotypes mostly arising from racist policies and ideologies. Black women during the Civil War and even today have been called "Jezebels"—constant sexual pleasure-seekers who therefore cannot be victims of rape or abuse. The stereotypical image of Latin American women is the hot-blooded dancing bar girl, "Carmen Miranda" or "hot tamale." Native American women are seen as the sexually uninhibited "squaws" who give their love freely to white men.[1] Pacific Islander women are affected also. Hollywood's representation gave American culture the image of "smiling, sarong-clad South Seas maidens with undulating hips."[2] Even white women a century ago were confined to the role of wife, mother or mistress.

Many of the racist stereotypes of Asian women and men were conceived during the yellow-peril hysteria of the late 1800s. Many Americans were fearful of the influx of Asians. In films, Asian women were shown as either cruel and cunning or quiet and submissive. One of the most prevalent stereotypical images of Asian women is the "dragon lady." The actress Anna May Wong, in 1920s films like *The Thief of Baghdad, Daughter of the Dragon* and *Shanghai Express,* best personified the image. Dragon ladies were portrayed as evil, conniving Asian villains who used their charm and beauty to seduce unsuspecting men.[3] Many decades later, films like *Sky Captain and the World of Tomorrow* and television shows like *Ally McBeal* continue to portray Asian women as dragon ladies. Bai Ling in the *Sky Captain* film plays a silent but menacing presence who symbolizes violence and impending evil. Ling Woo, played by Lucy Liu on *Ally McBeal,* is the sly and callous law firm dominatrix.

On the opposite end of the spectrum, Asian American women are portrayed as petite and subservient. She goes by other names: China doll, geisha girl. These images rose out of our wartime history. After World War II, the War Brides Act of 1945 allowed American military men to bring their wives and family over as immigrants. As a result, between 1945 and 1975 thousands of Chinese, Japanese and Filipina wives accompanied their military husbands to the United States.[4] The Asian war bride was seen as nonaggressive, compliant and sexually available, easily domesticated for American life. American men saw them as the epitome of womanhood—to the dismay of white American women. The China doll and the geisha girl evoke pictures of quiet, docile, overly feminine women whose main role is to please and serve men. These images emphasize the physical body over intelligence or voice. What is conveyed is that Asian women are useful only to serve, to be looked at or to be sexually exploited.

Another stereotype that plagues both men and women in the Asian American community is the model minority myth. The myth says that because Asian Americans are hardworking and highly educated, they over-

BEYOND THE STEREOTYPES

As a native Hawaiian woman who grew up in Hawai'i, attended a school with other children and young adults all of native Hawaiian ancestry, and participated in a hula halau (school of traditional Hawaiian dance), I am thankful to have had positive role models and affirmation of my identity as kanaka maoli ("true person" or native Hawaiian). During my college years and beyond, I've had many crosscultural experiences, and often I've experienced stereotyping because of my ancestry or ethnic identity. The struggle was magnified in settings where I was clearly a minority in majority culture. The experience brought up and continues to bring up insecurities, particularly when I sense judgment because of my perspective and worldview, styles of expression and cultural values. Over time I have sought to articulate these feelings and to push through by adapting (especially to Western styles of learning) while holding on to my cultural

values and ethnic identity in the process. It has been difficult. I find myself resisting internally when I feel others' expectation that I will assimilate in order to become "more successful," gain power and be taken seriously. I've had many encounters with people who with the greatest intentions have assumed that I like Hawai'i as romanticized by Hollywood (glamorous hula girls, spending every day at the beach, a beautiful paradise with no problems) or have tried to defend this stereotyping (these stereotypes are not offensive because they are separate from Hawaiian culture, its roots and its people).

It is very painful for me to see our culture exploited. I find that especially because I am kanaka maoli, I need to be intentional and prayerful about the way I speak to others about issues specifically concerning the native Hawaiian people and past or present injustices or oppression, because many times I've felt that people have stereotyped me as just another "angry Hawaiian"—and this causes them to not engage in the topic of concern. Because it is something so dear to my heart, it can be very discouraging, disappointing and hurtful when the response is not positive. It keeps me reliant on God and desperate to depend on and rest in him. It also makes me aware of the importance of partnership, crosscultural relationships and advocacy.

MOANI SITCH

come all barriers to succeed. Much of majority culture and many Asians themselves buy into the myth. This stereotype is potentially harmful because it pits Asians against other minority groups, who are conversely viewed as lazy or uneducated. Jane Hyun, author of *Breaking the Bamboo Ceiling,* writes that the model minority myth also "ignores the realities of subtle racism and discrimination faced by Asian Americans in the work place."[5] In addition, the myth also excludes Asians from the special assistance and funding offered by schools, companies or the government. Their voices are rarely heard in diversity discussions. Further, the stereotype puts Asian Americans under tremendous pressure to fulfill unrealistic expectations in school and in the workplace.

THE SILVER LINING

How the media and popular culture depict Asian Americans is important because it affects not only how other ethnic groups view Asians but how Asians view themselves. Although Asian American representation in the media over the years has been both lacking and negative, there have been a growing number of more positive images of women in recent years. Names like Indra K. Nooyi or Andrea Jung are not household names to many Americans yet. But they soon may be. Nooyi, of Asian Indian descent, is the newly elected CEO of PepsiCo. Andrea Jung, a Chinese American, serves as the chief executive of Avon. Both women are characterized as highly strategic, imaginative, nononsense, insightful and direct. They defy the stereotype of the docile, subservient Asian women, while still being wives and mothers. Currently, Nooyi will join Jung as only two of eleven Fortune 500 female executives. As Asian American women, they serve as role models for women, especially for women of color who dream about succeeding and leading in the marketplace.

In film, characters like Shu Lien (played by Michelle Yeoh) in *Crouching Tiger, Hidden Dragon,* portray Asian women as honorable and strong. Shu Lien is the woman warrior in love with Li Mu Bai (played by Chow Yun Fat). Her strength in swordsmanship is equally matched by her strength of character. She displays grace as she serves guests and dignitaries in her home, and she also possesses the moral character to honorably sacrifice her chance at love with Li Mu Bai for propriety's sake.

Another area where Asian American women are displaying influence is at the television news desk. Since Connie Chung's rise to fame on the *CBS Evening News with Dan Rather,* we are hard pressed to find a major metropolitan or local news network without at least one Asian American woman at the news desk. For some the prevalence of Asian American women is a sign of progress; for others, it signals a not-so-positive development. Professor

Darrell Hamamoto, author of *Monitored Peril: Asian Americans and the Politics of TV Representation,* proposes sexual politics as a reason for the growing numbers of Asian women as television anchors. According to Hamamoto, network execs feel that women of color are pleasing to television viewers' eyes. They serve as window dressing to strengthen ratings.

Nevertheless, Chung's face on our television screens has also been a positive catalyst for other Asian American women to enter television journalism. Chung and the other female Asian American journalists have created a niche where in previous decades there was a lack of ethnic diversity on television news. These women not only paved the way for other women of color but have served as role models for Asian women. Despite Hamamoto's critique of the news media industry, the fact is we get to see women who look like us on the television. The presence of intelligent and articulate Asian women in the media is a victory for the Asian American community. We feel excitement and pride when we see Asian American women make it to prominent positions—Lea Salonga, who won a Tony for the controversial role of Kim in *Miss Saigon;* Jenny Ming, who currently serves as the CEO of Old Navy; Jhumpa Lahiri, Pulitzer Prize winner in fiction for *Interpreter of Maladies;* and World Champion figure skaters Kristi Yamaguchi and Michelle Kwan.

I remember sitting in my living room during the 2002 Winter Olympics and watching Michelle Kwan perform in the free skate event. My house was full of people. While everyone's eyes were glued to the television screen, it seemed every Asian woman watching was on the edge of her seat. None of us had Olympic potential, so our hopes were set on Michelle. Our eyes intently followed her routine, up and down the ice. Every time she performed a jump we held our breath, hoping she would land gracefully to relieve our fears.

When she fell, some gasped and others screamed. I looked around and saw a few eyes that began to tear. Michelle's face showed dejection and a forced smile. Our faces were blank. We all sat silently for the rest of her routine. Our hearts broke that night. We felt the disappointment and sadness of seeing one of "our own" fail to achieve her dreams.

When we see Asian Americans get promoted, we cheer. When they fall on the ice, we cry with them. Our Asian value of being a communal culture allows us to share both their successes and their failures. We feel solidarity with them because they have paid their dues. They are trailblazers for other Asians in places that were (or are still) dominated by other ethnic groups. Our joy for Asian American women is balanced by awareness of their great responsibility in their positions. They fight off critics, combat sexism or racism, and represent the Asian community to the rest of the world, whether they identify with Asians or not. It is no wonder we feel a great affinity toward other Asian women who are able to excel in their professions. If they can succeed, so can we.

THE EFFECTS TODAY

Stereotyping is prevalent in the marketplace. According to a study done by the Asian Pacific American Women's Leadership Institute, the race and gender stereotypes of the domineering dragon lady and the shy and submissive geisha girl have posed challenges to women moving up in leadership positions in their workplaces. Women in the study felt that management would diminish leadership opportunities if they believed the shy and submissive stereotype.[6] Often stereotypes twist our own Asian cultural values. When women employ the values of interdependence, speaking only when spoken to or showing deference for those who lead, we appear unsuited for strong leadership in business. We are seen as not ambitious enough, not entrepreneurial enough, too reserved and quiet. Veronica, a media supervisor for an advertising agency in New York City, talks about moving beyond stereotypes and cultural norms that might hinder opportunities for promotion.

> At some point, I'm going to have to forcefully show that I am not as quiet and "nice" as I seem, that I can be loud, that I can lead. At this point, my work ethic has gotten me a couple promotions. And actually, I had to break out from my cultural roots of "don't rock the boat," and ask for a promotion. That's not what they expected from me. I know other Asian colleagues who go many years without ever asking—and they don't get [a promotion] either.[7]

Veronica represents many women in the corporate world who are trying to move beyond stereotypes and understand how Asian cultural values work in a Western setting.

I work for a nonprofit Christian organization that works primarily on college campuses. My job requires meeting with local pastors and university administrative staff frequently. As in the corporate world, there is much networking to be done and a need to make a good first impression. Stereotypes have affected how I conduct myself as a leader in both church and college ministry settings. The demeanor of a few male pastors changed from the initial phone conversations to meeting in person. A businesslike relationship on the phone turns to an overly familiar relationship in person. Sometimes I hear the words "sweet" and "But you look so young" used. Would the pastors use these words in conversations with men in my same position? Probably not. The patronizing words undercut my authority, whether the pastors know it or not. The effect is that my leadership is defined by my size and youthful appearance, rather than my job experience. I feel as if my seven years of ministry are overlooked.

There are times too, though, when our struggle to be respected is in situations with Asian men. Jessica, a campus minister in Georgia, talks about an encounter with a pastor in her city:

> There have been times where I feel like I have no voice. I met with a pastor who was new to my area. He was coming to start a church and wanted to meet up to "partner together." When we met, he was very nice, but at the same time I felt belittled. I was a woman, a Taiwanese American woman, and he was a Korean pastor. He shared his vision, and I shared my thoughts and asked follow-up questions. In the end, he was going to do what he was going to do. Later I asked my Korean male supervisor to meet with the pastor, to speak on my behalf, because I honestly wasn't sure if the pastor respected me, my work or my thoughts.[8]

Jessica is a competent college ministry and church leader. Yet she felt unheard by the older Korean pastor. The pastor's interaction with her may have reflected interethnic prejudice between Asian groups, gender stereotypes about women in leadership and maybe even age issues. The complex interplay of the three contributed to her feeling disrespected or that her authority as a woman leader was not viewed as legitimate. At the same time, she had the gift of an advocate in her Korean supervisor who spoke on her behalf.

THE POWER OF NAMES

Sticks and stones can break our bones, but words, too, can harm us. As much as we want to believe that words and names spoken about us are never harmful, they have power to either build or tear down our character. Even the "good" stereotypes—being self-sufficient or always successful—hurt Asians who do not fit the mold. All stereotypes, whether good or bad, strip people of their God-given wholeness and humanity. They become one dimensional.

- Asians are good at math and science.
- Asians are quiet.
- Asian women make good wives.
- Asians can't speak English very well.
- Asians are hard workers who don't rock the boat (model minority myth).

For anyone who has suffered from being boxed in by stereotypes, it is healing and refreshing to know that God understands the power and value of names. As we look through the Scriptures, we see God rename those whose lives he transforms. He takes unhealthy, potentially destructive names spoken over people and gives new names that reflect the honor and dignity due them as people of God.

Today, parents look through books to find a name for their newborn if they cannot come up with one on their own. Naming is about creativity or what sounds good. But in the ancient world, naming was much weightier. Names were well thought out to reflect blessings or curses on descendants. People used names to commemorate events or to remember the work of the Lord in their lives. In Genesis 17, God changed the names of Abram (exalted father) and Sarai (princess) to Abraham (father of many) and Sarah (popu-larly thought to mean princess of multitudes). God changed their names to signal the covenant he was making with them. He chose them to be both fa-ther and mother of many nations, with descendants more numerous than the stars in the sky and the sand on the shore. By renaming them, God showed his loving reign over their lives. He changed their identity from no-mads and sojourners to faithful followers of his promise. By taking their new given names, they reaffirmed their commitment and obedience to God to follow wherever he led.

We see the power of words and names in Mark 5, in the story of a woman who suffered from an ongoing menstruation for twelve years. Besides the physical pain and discomfort of such a long illness, she was socially ostra-cized. Jewish religious law deemed women with her condition as unclean and unfit to operate normally in society. The law stated that anyone who touched her or anyone she touched would be considered ceremonially un-clean. Jewish people, especially men, avoided her so as not to "catch" her uncleanness. I cannot imagine the loneliness her condition had caused for most of her adult life. Passersby saw her as unclean, outcast, poor and lonely.

All those labels did not stop her from taking desperate measures to gain healing. She broke all the religious cleanliness laws and went out into the open to see Jesus. She made her way into the crowd that massed around him. When she was close enough, she strained and reached out to touch the very edge of Jesus' robe, as if reaching for dear life.

At that moment, as her fingertips touched his dusty robe, she felt healing surge through her body. She knew instantly that her bleeding and twelve years of suffering stopped.

Jesus instantly felt power leave his body. With a large crowd pressing around him, I always wondered why Jesus chose to make a scene about this seemingly insignificant woman who had barely touched the hem of his robe. He asked out loud, "Who touched me?"

The woman, knowing that she would be exposed for breaking cleanliness laws and touching a rabbi, of all people, fell at the feet of Jesus. Trembling

STEREOTYPED OVERSEAS

Though I have felt stereotyped in subtle and insidious ways in the States, stereotypes took on a new and more obvious form when I moved overseas. Many things happened to me in the Middle East that would have made me angry in the States: adult strangers making slanty eyes at me, people asking if I ate worms, children yelling, "Japan, Japan!" at me, and the comments of strangers when they did not think I could understand their language. Every day I faced a choice: will I move on and let it go or stay upset? Unwanted attention and the ignorance of strangers stretched me in extending grace toward others and pushed me to find my identity in God. It helped me to identify with Jesus, who was misunderstood by most of the people with whom he came into contact (Is 53:3). Sometimes even his closest friends did not understand his true identity or the purpose of his life.

One of the many blessings for me of being a bicultural person in mission was that it rooted me much more deeply in my identity as an adopted child of our heavenly Father (Eph 1:5). When my identity as an Asian American and a missionary (a taboo word in a Muslim country) and my role as a woman were challenged, there was one firm and foundational truth that I could turn to—my primary identity is not my ethnicity, my job or role, or even my gender. My primary identity is a beloved child of the Father. I would remind myself of this as I walked through the bazaar or felt the stare of children. I am a daughter of the King of kings, I would tell myself.

CHRISTINE

with fear, she confessed the whole situation. While the crowd would expect Jesus to scold her for wasting his time or for breaking Jewish law, Jesus used the opportunity to further her healing. He said to her, "Daughter, your faith has made you well; go in peace, and be healed of your disease" (Mk 5:34).

Daughter. When was the last time someone had referred to her with such loving and fatherly language? For the past twelve years, the woman's condition had been a widening chasm between her and the community. Now the name *daughter* served as a bridge to bring her back into the community. The beloved Messiah called this woman back into relationship with him and with the town. The years of suffering and loneliness ended the moment Jesus spoke to her for all to hear. Moreover, he highlighted her faith in front of the whole crowd. The former outcast was now an insider. She would be known from then on as faithful, healed, free and, most important, a daughter of the King.

Jesus can redeem women from the negative labels others put on us. No one ever expected Jesus to gladly receive the bleeding woman and restore her to society. Yet he did so, willingly. What are the labels that have been put on us? Jesus sees beyond the dragon ladies and China dolls. He reaches out to us as we reach for him. He wants us to take the hurts, the labels put on us, and give us a new way of living. There is great power in knowing who Christ made us to be.

- We are made in the image of God (Gen 1:27).
- We are fearfully and wonderfully made (Ps 139:14).
- We will not be put to shame (Is 54:4).
- We are God's chosen people (Col 3:12).
- We have the mind of Christ (1 Cor 2:16).
- We are called for God's purpose (Rom 8:28).
- We are given gifts by God (Rom 12:6).

We need to ask God to help us embrace these truths about him, his power and our identity in him. Letting these truths soak into us is a process. As we begin to meditate on these words and let them take root in our mind and heart, we see their power to protect us from the lies of stereotypes. The truths of Scripture make the power of Asian stereotypes hollow. I thank God that we are more than sweet faces and silent tea servers. I can rest in the truth that Jesus calls me by a new name.

OUR RESPONSE

Knowing our true identity as God's daughters is the first step in dispelling Asian stereotypes. As we live in the awareness that old names and stereotypes have no power over us, we can look for creative ways to empower Asian American women and challenge the landscape of the media, the workplace and the church. Here are a few ways to respond to the stereotypes that confront us.

Use our voices for others and ourselves. One of the most powerful ways to respond is to use our God-given voice. A senior Asian American male in my organization counseled an audience of Asian men and women to speak up when necessary. When we hear racial slurs or stereotypes made about us or other groups, let's not be afraid to lovingly correct friends, colleagues or supervisors. We have the responsibility and opportunity to correct misperceptions that others have of Asians.

Recently in a Christian conference setting, a white American woman inadvertently uttered a racial slur about Chinese people. A colleague of mine, shocked and perturbed, decided to use her voice on behalf of Chinese people, even though she herself was not Chinese. She mustered up the courage to teach the woman why terms like *chinaman* are racist and hurtful.

My Asian American women friends have used their collective voice to begin letter-writing campaigns on behalf of Asians and other ethnic minority groups. One wrote to a local newspaper that had misrepresented Asians in an article. She highlighted the one-dimensional way the writer spoke of Asians in education and challenged the paper to expand the "Asian" category to other Southeast Asian groups, like Thai, Vietnamese and Filipino.

In the work setting, career coach Jane Hyun advises us to hold our ground in conversations. As Asian women work within companies and organizations whose management style is Western and where assertiveness is valued, holding our ground gains us more respect. Though this goes against our deep value of respecting authority, we can begin to learn when to abide by our cultural norms and when to lay them aside for a time. When we de-

I am Chinese American, and I grew up in Staten Island, New York (predominantly Caucasian but recently has been seeing an influx of Asians). I would say that I didn't have very much pride in being Asian, as very few of my school friends were Asian until I went to Stuyvesant High School, where suddenly it was "cool" to be Asian. In my elementary and junior high years, I had grown bitter and even hateful of my classmates because of name calling in reference to my Asian background. It wasn't until I became a Christian my senior year of high school that I could truly forgive them and be free of that hurt and anger.

I feel that spending my high school and college years, and now postcollege years, in New York City have really influenced my feelings about my ancestry and my acceptance of God's role for me. I see now that the years of struggle I had in accepting my race only help me to identify with persons of other cultures who may feel like they are second class.

When I went to Pine Ridge, South Dakota, to serve the Lakota Sioux, I talked with people and heard about their experiences with racism. I felt that I could identify with that, having been discriminated against in the classroom by my peers. As the only ethnic minority member of my team (who were predominantly from the Midwest and "all American"), I felt blessed. The bad experiences from my childhood were somehow being redeemed through my ability to empathize and connect to the Native Americans I met there.

JOANNA CHEN

fault to speaking rather than staying silent, we help pave the way to a more inclusive and culturally aware work environment.

Look for training and growing opportunities. Growing in leadership skills helps us to break out of the boxes of stereotypical images. InterVarsity

Christian Fellowship, a national nonprofit Christian organization, sponsors the Daniel Project, a leadership course that develops its Asian American staff for management positions. This leadership course follows a trend among many companies: to develop emerging leaders. Through the Daniel Project I learned how to use my voice and speak up in work settings; the value of seeking mentors and advocates; and the art of "managing up"—learning to communicate ideas and needs to managers and supervisors. Such programs not only allow Asian Americans to dream about how we want to move up within our organizations but also give us the tools to achieve the dreams. Churches, too, can invest in leadership programs to train members to take more active roles in ministry. Talk with your pastor to learn about his or her leadership vision for men and women, and see how you can get involved.

THE HOPE

As we become more adept at counteracting stereotypes, we actually *become* the positive examples that we long to see. As more capable, confident Asian American women gain prominence within the business world, government, church and media, younger Asian American women will have role models who inspire them. Although it may take years to completely undo the effects of stereotypes, the visibility and voices of prominent Asian American women can shift the general public's assumptions and associations regarding what Asian American women are like. We are talented, creative and influential women from whom all society can learn.

My hope is that in the coming years our picture of the Asian American woman will transform. When a little girl watches a movie and sees an Asian American actress, she won't feel shame or embarrassment but will feel excited and proud. When a young woman watches a news program with an Asian American anchorwoman, she will feel validated and empowered. Or when we see Asian American women CEOs, we will say to ourselves, *I can do that, too!* We are more than diminutive, exotic and submissive. We do more than serve tea. As God restores our true names—*daughter, beloved, chosen* and *leader*—may we use our names and gifts to influence the world around us.

Hello
Somewhere between
Isle girl
billowing hips
welcome to paradise
a smile, a hibiscus
holding back cascades
sun-browned black hair
and
kanaka maoli
angry advocate
wounded scream
exploited land
displaced people
lost sovereignty
I see my name.

2

Pulled by Expectations

KATHY KHANG

*F*rom the moment I grabbed the pencil off the table on my first birthday, I was raised to know, understand and live up to the expectations of my family and culture.

Korean custom dictates that a child's destiny is determined or made known on the first birthday at the *dol-jabee,* a ceremony in which the child is allowed freedom to pick up any of several items symbolizing things like wealth and longevity. My parents and I had recently immigrated to the United States. After months of transitions and uncertainty, my first birthday was an occasion for celebration. My parents invited everyone they knew to attend my first birthday party and watch me "choose" my future.

So they sat me down in front of the table set with things like money, symbolizing wealth, and string, symbolizing longevity, and without a moment's hesitation I grabbed the pencil. From then on I was expected to excel in academics.

If only life's expectations had remained that simple. With every year and stage of development came new expectations. Through the grade school years it wasn't enough to be a good student. My parents expected me to learn to speak, read and write Korean, because I was Korean before I was American. My friends thought it was weird that I went to Korean language school. When high school came, my parents and I heard the best colleges were looking for well-rounded students, so we all expected me to join the choir and the pom-pom squad, take advanced-placement biology, and help teach Sunday school at church. What we didn't expect were the awkward conversations about the turnabout dance or homecoming or prom—words and concepts I wasn't sure existed in Korean language and culture. When college came, I was expected to do well academically, find some nice Korean Christian friends, and go home on weekends to help at my parents' business and attend my "home" church. My non-Asian American friends could not understand the power my parents seemed to have over me.

EXPECTATIONS FROM BOTH EAST AND WEST

Asian American women straddle multiple worlds and often filter conflicting messages and expectations. The East values hierarchy and patriarchy, community and family, harmony and indirect communication. The West embraces egalitarian structures and partnerships, gender equality and individualism, confrontation and direct communication.

The Asian daughter is dutiful and often silent. The Western daughter is allowed personal space and voice. In some Asian cultures, married women traditionally keep their "maiden" surname because culturally they are not considered a member of the new family but rather a piece of property. In Western culture, the woman can choose to keep her maiden name for convenience or to make a statement.

We know very well what it's like to live with family expectations breathing down our backs:

Get married! (and to the right man)
Have children! (meaning more than one)
Make money! (and lots of it)
Can't you be like _____? (Fill in the blank with the name of your nerd cousin, valedictorian friend or other mother-appointed rival.)

PHOEBE ENG

The Asian mother sacrifices everything for her children, especially her sons, and she often swallows sorrow as if it were aspirin. The Western mother sacrifices everything for her children and, according to the popular television show *Desperate Housewives*, often swallows wine or her child's Ritalin to cope.

A beautiful Asian woman is one who has fair skin with Western features—big eyes, bigger breasts and a nose bridge to rest a pair of trendy eye-glasses on. A beautiful American woman means being airbrushed, nipped and tucked to perfection—wrinkle-free skin, bigger breasts and sometimes a smaller nose. Life becomes increasingly complex when the values of the Asian and the American fuse together into an impossible ideal.

As the Asian American landscape continues to change, so do the expectations. Asian immigrants looking for academic and economic opportunities came in waves as immigration quotas shifted after World War II and again in the 1970s and 1980s. There have also been waves of Asian immigrants fleeing their countries but bringing with them their agrarian lifestyle and values. The Hmong in the United States have come mainly from Laos as refugees from the Vietnam War. The Hmong were farmers in their homeland and were recruited by the U.S. government to fight there; when Vietnam fell to communism, many fled their homeland in fear of persecution. They brought with them a tradition of large families, unlike the more recent immigrants from China, where a one-child policy limits family size. Hmong culture relied on and celebrated large families, and women played a key role by marrying young to bear children.

At a conference for young Hmong leaders held in Whitewater, Wisconsin, Hmong American women discussed the special challenges they face. Their parents' expectation that they will marry young to start a large family flies in the face of their opportunities for higher education and a career. Going to college to pursue a career, delaying marriage and the possibility of being a working mom are new concepts that put them in uncharted cultural territory.

Hollywood's visual representation of Amy Tan's novel *The Joy Luck Club* gave voice to the Asian American woman's experience. Reading the novel was an intimate experience for me, as the words resonated with the oral history my mother and grandmothers had passed down.

But when the story hit the silver screen, it was not bigger than life but rather just like real life. For the first time on screen, America saw Asian American women and their mothers, fathers, daughters and friends eat, laugh, cry and live out the culture clash. Viewers interacted with the stories of the four daughters, their mothers, and the sometimes toxic and sometimes freeing ways the fictional characters walked in both worlds.

A key theme in the film was how the older generation's own brokenness and disappointments evolved into hopes and expectations for future generations. Asian American women carry the weight of not only our own expectations but those of our mothers and their mothers and their mothers' mothers. Just as in the movie, they say they don't *expect* things, only *hope,* but the weight of their hopes can be discouraging if not deeply painful at times. We cannot be and do what they hope for.

But what if what our parents are hoping for is something—or worse, someone—we can never, ever be? There isn't enough room in the top universities for all of us. Not all of us could possibly become doctors or lawyers. There aren't enough perfect Asian American men for all of us to marry. But what if the expectations we fail to meet aren't the schools we attend, the majors we choose, career paths we follow, or whether or not we marry?

For some of us the deepest pain is being a daughter and failing to meet the cultural expectation to be a son. Cultures once deeply agrarian needed, literally, manpower. Women were not always valued or celebrated—they were simply necessary for their role in producing the family heirs. The cultural preference for boys continues to deeply affect Asian American women like Christina.

A twenty-seven-year-old Chinese American, Christina grew up in Virginia without consciously realizing how much the cultural preference for sons affected her. But now she recalls that when her youngest sibling was born—a boy—her mother remarked on how sad it was that Christina's grandmother had died before seeing the birth of a grandson.

"It made me sad for my mom, because she probably felt the need to have a son to make her mother happy—a cascading brokenness. In my head I know the preference, so in that sense I understand it. In my heart I don't understand it. But what really impacted me was that my mom said it as if that was just the way it was—that boys are more valuable. I wonder if my mom doesn't see herself as being as valuable as her brothers."

Christina's desire to meet her parents' expectations was rooted in her need to have value and worth. *If only I could do and be what they want, I would be as valuable as a son.*

As Asian American daughters of the King, we cannot be driven by hopes and desires tangled in culture and family ties, lest our desires to please and meet those expectations become like idols—graven images of the perfect Asian American daughter, sister, student, campus leader, Sunday school teacher, wife, mother, professional, which we spend a lifetime worshiping.

Expectations can become a dark drive pushing me to the brink of perfectionism. My parents expected me to do well in school, but they never said they wanted me to consume insane amounts of caffeine and deprive my body of sleep and rest. My husband and children expect and want my love and attention, but they have never said they want me to be so busy making the house into our home that I have no time to spend with them. My supervisor expects me to grow in my skills as a supervisor, but she has never said she wants me to put my job over my family. I've too often internalized expectations only after translating them into impossible, unhealthy and ungodly expectations.

GOD'S PLAN

God's intention was for us to *be* and *do;* he gave us form and function, creating a place and purpose for us. Adam and Eve were given the Garden of Eden as a place to be and become. They were given a place, and their relationships were all in harmony and balance.

In Genesis 1 and 2 we read the creation account and see how our Lord, the Creator, forms and fills the universe. God first creates the space and place and then declares, "Let us make humankind in our image, according to our likeness; and let them have dominion over the fish of the sea, and over the birds of the air, and over the cattle, and over all the wild animals of the earth, and over every creeping thing that creeps upon the earth" (Gen 1:26). God creates human beings in his image, male and female, charging us to "fill the earth and subdue it" (Gen 1:28).

First and foremost the desire and intention laid out by the Architect himself is that we are to be reflections of him. He creates us to be in relationship with him and with one another, and then he gives us our roles—our work—as a blessing and privilege, as we are the only creatures created in his image.

In the best moments of living in a broken world, we women taste a bit of what the Lord intended for us: We enter a room filled with family and friends for a special celebration; there are conversations to be had, food to feast on and company to enjoy. But quickly, those moments fall apart when often-competing pressures—the expectations of our family and community—collide in full force.

Say hello to all the elders of the family, making a beeline for my maternal grandmother, my parents, and my aunties and uncles. Don't forget to acknowledge and provide "big sister" support and encouragement to my younger cousins. Help prepare and serve the food while making sure my husband is settled in with a plate of appetizers and a drink. Oh, and the children should be well behaved and entertained as my well-coiffed, well-heeled self wends gracefully through the chaos, hoping to actually be a part of the celebrating, enjoying it, before it devours me.

It seems I'm supposed to be so many things to so many people. It's easy to internalize very deeply the expectations of the world around me and identify so closely with my failures to meet those expectations that I forget who God created me to be—a reflection of him.

The *Oprah Winfrey Show* has a running spot called "The Wildest Dreams Tour" in which Oprah and her crew grant some unsuspecting viewer's wildest dreams. My husband and I talked about a segment we saw, and I knew exactly what his wildest dream would be. As a dutiful, loving wife, I am expected to know that he would want a large sum of money and a large chunk of time to write, direct and produce a movie.

But when it was my turn to share my wildest dream, I was speechless. I couldn't come up with some crazy dream worthy of Oprah's attention. And it annoyed me.

My husband, Peter, calmly responded, "Well, honey, you spend all of your time thinking about and caring for others. You don't have dreams for yourself."

I know exactly what the world and culture expect of me—the firstborn daughter, older sister, wife of a firstborn son, mother of three, and supervisor. What do I expect of myself? What do I expect *for* myself? Wouldn't that be selfish and unspiritual?

Is it possible to live up to other people's expectations or even my own distorted expectations? Am I saying no to things that actually I should say yes to? In the noise of life, as we juggle relationships and expectations, it is difficult to discern and decide what to choose and how to make those choices.

Yet stilling myself long enough to hear from God about his hopes and dreams for me is hardly unspiritual or selfish. It's exactly what we need to do in order to silence the noise of our lives. It's what I'm created to do. When I think about it, I know God wants me to be there, in his presence, in relationship with him, listening to him, dreaming with him.

CHOOSING WHAT IS BETTER

Did God make a mistake blessing us with a culture so rich and roles so incredible? Absolutely not. However, somewhere in the "progress" of modernity and technological "advances" that are supposed to help us live our lives running 24/7, we've forgotten God's intention in the many roles we play.

The roles God has given me become distorted when I stop using Scripture to help me filter through the expectations. What I do instead is run.

By the time the two older kids are at school and I am back home with my youngest, it's about 9:00 a.m. I settle down with a cup of coffee and my favorite breakfast. It would be the perfect time to sit with God and his Word, but more often than not it is the time to sit with the morning paper or today's to-do list. Years before I was a working mom, I would run from God during such moments, fearing that God had more expectations of me. In college, the moments that would have been ripe to meet with God and enjoy his presence were often filled with procrastination—shuffling papers, highlighting every other line in my textbooks, reading the syllabi. *God must expect something more from me,* I thought, and I was afraid those expectations, and the guilt and shame of not meeting them, would send me over the edge.

It wasn't until I grasped Luke 10:38-42 that I became free to sit and become more of who God intended and less of what the world expected.

Martha and Mary remind me a lot of another modern-day Martha (Stewart), who runs a multimillion-dollar set of enterprises in the homemaking industry. It's a good thing to have a magazine, television show, radio spot and so on to give us an outline for living the good-enough-for-a-magazine-shoot sort of life, but the biblical Martha already fell for that trick.

The picture we see is a familiar one. Martha either had the gift of hospitality or understood that when an important person came to town you opened your home. There were male guests waiting to be served and two women on the scene.

Martha wasn't doing anything unusual or alarming. She was doing exactly what you or I would be expected (and would expect ourselves) to do. There was rice to be made, dishes to prepare, chai and samosas to serve. The house should be clean, and everything should be ready to make it a pleasant visit for the guests. She was fulfilling the cultural and social expectations that have become timeless.

It was Mary's response that is alarming and disturbing. She sat. And she didn't just sit, as she would have when hiding or being lazy. She sat at Jesus' feet—not exactly where you would expect any woman to be. She placed herself where only men were culturally expected and allowed to have been—at the feet of their teacher. Women were not permitted to be religious students, but Mary took such a posture.

Martha was "distracted by her many tasks" (Lk 10:40) and noticed that her sister wasn't fulfilling expectations. Martha continued to fulfill what she valued and understood most deeply—cultural values and expectations. She approached Jesus, who was the authority figure, and asked for his help.

Jesus' response should stop us in our tracks and silence us. "Martha, Martha, you are worried and distracted by many things; there is need of only one thing. Mary has chosen the better part, which will not be taken away from her" (Lk 10:41-42).

Jesus set the record straight. Culturally, it was assumed that a guest's physical needs for food and water took precedence, so that was what Martha set out to do. But Jesus was telling Martha that her relationship with him, sitting at his feet, comes before running around and doing. He was not telling Martha to stop being a Middle Eastern Jewish woman. He is not telling me to forget that I am an Asian American woman, wife, mother of three very active children, daughter, daughter-in-law, sister, sister-in-law and professional. He was not telling Martha that a meal was never necessary, nor is he telling me that it's OK to forget to feed my family. Jesus was not even telling Martha she made a wrong choice or a bad choice. Jesus *is*, however, telling us that the order of our lives should be that *our relationship with him comes first.*

Jesus was not surprised by Martha's actions. He knew she was worried and upset. He expected that. But he also expected a relationship that requires sitting still and silencing our own powerful agendas despite our time's cultural norms.

Mary's response was not that of the passive, quiet, exotic girl who sits with a demure smile covered by her hands. She was not sitting in protest or in anger against society's expectations of her. She was not wrong. She sat at Jesus' feet in a radical, countercultural statement, proclaiming quite publicly that she was a disciple of Jesus. And Jesus welcomed her radical act of obedience, even as it flew in the face of cultural expectations.

Just like Mary, we need to still ourselves at Jesus' feet—to learn to say no or even "not right now" to the things that pull us away (or allow us to run away) from saying yes and being open to the better things. We need to work through the expectations and issues that keep us from being disciples of Jesus.

Mary chose the better thing. She chose to declare that she was a disciple first, despite the cultural norms and expectations that were driving Martha to the brink of anger and perhaps neurosis. Mary chose to sit when it would have been easier and more socially acceptable to run around serving Jesus and the "real" disciples. Mary did not argue her choice or try to be something she was not. She sat down and listened.

Jesus calls us into relationship with him not to give us another list of expectations we cannot meet, but to walk with us, to give us wisdom and discernment to know what and when to do, and to give us the grace, courage and freedom to say no to other things.

Do I choose first to run to—or away from—the many roles the Lord has called me to? Or do I first choose to be his disciple? Unless I spend time with the Lord, how will I know to what or whom he is calling me?

For us, the challenge isn't rejecting our culture—East or West.

Part of the blessing of living in multiple cultural worlds is that it opens up multiple cultural worlds for us to access and learn from.

Shawna grew up in Seattle. As a biracial woman, she had two cultural pictures of what it meant to be a woman. Her Grandma Campbell used to sit on her husband's lap. That was something that her Japanese grandmother would never do. But these two pictures of what women could be like provided her with more options. Sometimes she adopts her Japanese side's more reserved posture. But she feels free to choose to be more affectionate or emotionally open when that is appropriate. Both sides are a part of who she is.

The Asian in me compels me to seek counsel from my community. My family and friends know me and love me enough to gently rebuke me when perfectionism takes a hold on my life and hurts my family and community. The American in me gives me the freedom to say "no, thank you" to the things I'm not gifted in or called to; living in the land of opportunities does not mean I have to take advantage of them all. The Christian in me reminds me there is more to life than pursuing the American Dream.

"Choosing the better thing" means embracing a completely new paradigm defined first by God. Will you and I be obedient first to the Lord by fully engaging in a relationship with him? Or will we first run to fulfill the expectations of the world and of our cultures, hoping only later that he will recognize and bless our futile efforts?

Will you choose first to be an excellent student, a campus leader, a girlfriend, a daughter, to find value? Or will you sit at Jesus' feet and choose first the better thing? Are you a Christian who happens to be a student/daughter/

girlfriend? Or are you a student/daughter/girlfriend who happens to be a Christian? What comes first?

I haven't yet figured it out. I am more often than not Martha—with an electric rice cooker, microwave, laptop and cell phone. And while the trappings of the modern world make it easier to make dinner and to multitask, they also make it easier to run away from Jesus than to sit at his feet.

Just the other day, my husband told my supervisor that his one concern about my role as a middle manager was that the line between home and office too often blurs into a string of "just one more e-mail, honey"s. She appropriately responded by asking Peter if that workaholic behavior is rooted in the job description or in the choices I make. Am I trying to meet an actual job expectation, or am I trying to find my value in my job?

So what does it look like to choose the better thing?

Sometimes it means making your parents unhappy. Sarah, a thirty-six-year-old Vietnamese American, said the struggle between honoring her parents and following the call and path God has for her has often meant wres-

The American Dream—a life of hope, opportunities and freedom—is exactly what Sarah's family wanted and needed. Sarah and her family left Vietnam on April 20, 1975—the day Saigon fell to the communist regime. Sarah's family fled Vietnam fearing persecution because of family ties to a rice factory that supplied the U.S. government. They could not expect or even hope for a future in Vietnam.

Sarah was five at the time, the youngest of four children. The family left by boat and spent several months at a refugee camp in southern California before being relocated to the Pacific Northwest.

Living up to our parents' expectations of a successful, happy life can seem like a nonnegotiable when they've given up everything to provide safety as well as opportunities. But the tension of conflicting cultural values came to a head for Sarah in 1995, when she was diagnosed with lupus just a few months after her wedding.

"We were all just coming out of college. We had our whole lives ahead of us—career-driven ambitions," she recalls.

But the disease left her weak, physically unable to do what she herself expected. She cut back her hours as a research analyst and later found out that she had been passed over for a promotion to become a program manager because she had fallen off the career track's expectations.

"I felt like a failure," she said. She had failed to meet the career expectations that would redeem her parents' costly journey. Lupus took more than her career goals—her own expectations as a woman and a wife came into question. Treatment included chemotherapy, and as the treatments were putting the disease into remission, they were also ending her chances of conceiving.

"What does it mean to be a woman? I always thought it was being able to bear a child, and not being able to do it, not even having the option, was devastating. It was the idea of what I always envisioned for myself—you get married, you have children," she said.

While wrestling with disappointment and unmet expectations, Sarah's parents communicated love and care for her. But it came wrapped in a sense that her life now fell short. Her parents, drawing on the Buddhist influence in Vietnamese culture, often wondered if something they had done, some wrong they or Sarah had committed in the past, was the root cause of her illness.

It forced Sarah to ask God the hard questions. *Are you punishing me? If I do something, change something, can I get healthy? Can I have a baby?* And in the hard questions, God loved Sarah and gave her a deeper understanding of his love.

"It's not God punishing me. It's not anything we've done right or wrong. You don't have to earn this or earn that. In the end, it's kind of been easier to let go because I'm recognizing God's unconditional love for me. There are other opportunities for me, and that was just one of them."

tling with and then giving up feelings of guilt for falling short of her parents' expectations. In college, Sarah headed down the pre-med route at an elite Big Ten private university, but she fell short when she decided medical school wasn't the direction God had in mind.

"Especially as part of an immigrant family, you feel like you owe your parents so much. I feel like I need to make them happy. I'm so indebted to them. But there is this fine line, and I realized that I am not responsible for them being happy. I do want them to be happy, but that is not my responsibility. I can't make them happy," she said.

For a season of my life, choosing what is better has meant saying no to opportunities to serve and meet a need at church because my husband and I have decided life is too full right now. Sometimes it's letting the laundry wait an hour while I spend some time with Jesus.

More often than not, it is not as easy as yes or no. Much like mastering the subtleties inherent in many Asian languages, choosing the better thing takes wisdom and patience in order to honor our culture and follow Jesus.

Choosing the better thing is always being a student of Jesus, just as Mary's posture at Jesus' feet indicated her desire to learn. Growing up with consistent and strong lessons in Korean culture left me a confused, sometimes angry, sometimes voiceless young woman. But more recently, I have looked back at those lessons in serving tea and preparing meals in a very different light, as my father-in-law moved in with us shortly after the death of my mother-in-law. Actions I once thought only subservient and slightly annoying—using the most respectful degree of Korean language, serving meals to the oldest and the men first—have become ways of showing love and care and honor to my father-in-law, as well as ways of showing respect to my parents by living out what they taught me. More than just serving my father-in-law, I am finding that the choices God has called me to make—to embrace some cultural expectations I once despised—have opened up conversations with my father-in-law and my parents about other choices I've made that they've disagreed with. God is reshaping our cultural lens, opening up dialogue where there had been a wall of opposing expectations.

Choosing the better thing is knowing that when we say no or "not now" to doing acts of service to please others or to fulfill someone else's expectations, we do not become less valuable in God's eyes. We are always his precious daughters.

The way I live—the way we women in the tension of two cultures live— is absurd and borderline crazy. Choosing to be mommy or wife or middle manager isn't wrong. Choosing to be a doctor or teacher or business professional isn't wrong. What's wrong—where I, where we, fall into sin—is when our roles become our sole identity and eventually our idol.

Our cultural heritage can be a gift, even as we navigate through the expectations. In Asian culture, community has a high value. Our choices are not our own but are a reflection of our community, our family. So as a Christian Asian American woman, you are not alone as you wonder if your parents will ever be satisfied. You are not alone as you feel the tension. Turn to God, turn to close friends, turn to the wise aunties and Christian mentors in your family of faith. Invite others to help you resist cultural idols and live as a daughter of the King.

Will we choose first to fulfill the expectations of those around us and of our personal idols? Or will we first be at his feet choosing the better thing?

expecting
will you understand
(or will you require)
less than obedience
perfection
loyalty
less than the ideal
daughter
lover
friend
(or will you require?)
when can I rest
away from myself

3

Perfectionistic Tendencies

NIKKI A. TOYAMA

Look at me, I could never pass for a perfect bride, or a perfect daughter.

MULAN

I stood perfectly still next to my sister, the bride. As the maid of honor, I made sure she was OK and, more important, that her dress looked beautiful.

The ceremony began. That's when it decided to come out and taunt me. A small wrinkle appeared—the only flaw on the perfect dress. It grew with each move. I knew my mother, sitting directly behind, hadn't missed it. When the preacher paused, my sister handed me her bouquet. With one hand I grabbed the flowers. The other slid over the skirt. I smoothed out her dress. The wrinkle fled. The world returned to its natural equilibrium.

"Did you see the wrinkle?" my mother and I said almost simultaneously as soon as the ceremony ended. Her eyes had seen the crease before it dared to appear. We saw the one imperfection but did not notice all the lovely details— the vibrant red of the flowers or "Trumpet Voluntary" echoing through the church. My mother and I know the entire life history of that wrinkle.

I could tell you five things that are wrong with any situation, any performance, anything that I've done. It's instinctive. It's a lot harder to tell you what went right in the same situation.

At a recent ministry gathering, my supervisor asked one of the Japanese Americans if she knew origami. Earlier in the week, we had talked about culture, and he wanted to give each person an origami crane to take home as a reminder of the lesson. Of course Sharon knew origami. An origami crane is the quintessential Japanese-y trick to dazzle your friends during a boring lecture. So she gathered the other two Japanese Americans in the group, Collin and me, to help. We found origami paper and began to make seventy cranes. Between the three of us, we figured we could make the one-hour deadline.

The clock moved faster than our fingers. Eventually the stress showed on our faces—we were not going to finish in time. The three of us folded quickly. Despite the time pressure, each crane looked identical to the previous. We didn't know how to compromise quality for speed. There is no documented "acceptable flaw" for an origami crane. A good crane has clean lines, no rips, and perfectly parallel angles and creases. A picture of the ideal crane had rooted itself in my psyche early. The voices of aunties and grandmothers reinforced these strict rules. As we folded, we mimicked the little criticisms—"Oh, so sloppy!" "Too many creases!" "Be careful to align the edges." These small details were invisible to most, but we saw every fatal flaw.

My Caucasian friend Josh came up. With an earnest heart, he wanted to help. After he fumbled on his own, we could see he had missed some of the major details—his folds were not straight, his edges didn't line up. It would

Perfectionist versus	*Pursuit of Excellence*
Idealistic	*Realistic*
Strives for the impossible	*Strives for the doable*
Fears failure	*Anticipates success*
Dwells on mistakes	*Learns from mistakes*
Values self by what they do	*Values self by who they are*

Source: David Stoop, *Hope for the Perfectionist* (Nashville: Thomas Nelson, 1998). Used with permission.

have been too much work to walk him through values that were innate to us.

From then on poor Josh just watched as we labored and the deadline came and went. We didn't have time to nitpick and point out all the different flaws until Josh perfected each of his cranes. And something in us would not let us say, "This is how you do it; just try your best." None of us could bring ourselves to lower the standard of the crane—there wasn't an acceptable flaw. There was the perfect crane and nothing else. All this passed between us, unspoken but understood.

NO MISTAKES ALLOWED

All of my mistakes stand out. The 2 percent missed versus the 98 percent achieved. The A- that could have been an A. Yet I don't consider myself a perfectionist: my room is a mess, my filing system is nonexistent, and I don't care what my car looks like. As a child I walked out of the house with one ankle sock and one knee sock—I just didn't care. While I may not have the personality of a perfectionist, I carry a very strong cultural value for it.

Perfectionism is integrally woven into my Japanese culture. I see it in the care of the clerk in the stationery store wrapping my purchase. Beautiful wrapping paper, a small bow, a string tied perfectly and no tape showing. Even the corners have been pinched to form a sharp crease. Japanese culture has strict rules for seemingly mundane activities. When serving tea, hold your wrist just so. Whisk the tea like this. Hold the teapot as you pour, and hold back your sleeve. Japanese culture is filled with lots of little rules about everything—how to sit, to stand, to tie a knot, to laugh. Each activity has a proper way. These rules form the lens through which I see myself and others.

Unhealthy perfectionism goes beyond striving for excellence. The ideal is the ultimate goal. Coming close doesn't count; there is no A for effort. Perfectionism sets unrealistically high standards.[1] It is not unique to Asian culture; perfectionists live in every country of the world. But in many Asian communities there is a communal value for perfectionism. It's reinforced by how each group member functions and treats the others.

THE CULTURAL ROOTS

Making mistakes in isolation is hard in itself. But Asian cultures have two traits that make individual mistakes carry more than individual consequences. One of them is shame and its communal implications. Japanese culture, for example, is a shame-based culture. It's important to "save face" personally, but it is also important to help others save face. It feels very uncomfortable to watch someone else being humiliated, making a mistake and embarrassing themselves. Others might step in to avoid that situation. There's a strong dynamic of assuming that "your shame is my shame" because of the communal nature of Asian communities. In fact, friends or family members will publicly humiliate a deviant to separate themselves from the bad behavior and save face.

In China, people are taken to the street with placards around their necks confessing their mistakes and promising to reform—thus they are made negative examples for others. In Japan, the dishonorable samurai committed *seppuku*—ritual suicide. In this way, he took his shame with him and didn't taint his family or his lord. Such extreme examples communicate the seriousness of bringing shame on others. Individual choices have group consequences. Cultures that are both shame based and highly communal penalize individuals harshly for making mistakes.

The other factor that drives many Asians to perfectionism is the expectations of their parents or communities. Psychologists call this socially prescribed perfectionism. This type of perfectionism stems from the belief that significant people in others' lives hold high standards of achievement for them. Fear of rejection pushes perfectionist tendencies. Some are driven to perfectionism by others (socially prescribed) while others drive themselves (internally driven perfectionism). Whereas internally driven perfectionism has some positive effects (high execution, commitment), there is very little that is positive about socially prescribed perfectionism.[2]

Families may have rigid scripts for what is acceptable in their family or clan. A physical ideal is held up before a daughter—her ears are not attached, she's too tall, she has too many moles on her face, she's too fat, she's too dark, her eyes are too small. Many Asian women are killing themselves in the attempt to reach or maintain a certain physique.

If I was fat, I was invisible.
If I was thin, I was lovable.
MARGARET CHO, COMEDIENNE

tempt to reach or maintain a certain physique. Whether it's eating disorders, plastic surgery, spending lots of money on cosmetics or a constant dissatisfaction with their looks, many struggle yet are unable to attain a specific outward form of physical perfection. No amount of good can compensate for the one flaw.

The movie *Bend It Like Beckham* shows the perfection dynamic within a South Asian family in the United Kingdom. The bad behavior of a younger sister affects her older sister's engagement. The family asks, "Who will marry into such a family?" There's not a lot of grace when mistakes are made.

In the Filipino community, perfectionism may be expressed in the arts, in standards of beauty or in educational expectations. Families may have a script that was developed and handed down through the generations—a recipe for success. However, some of the demands for perfection may have other sources.

A few years ago, a speaker, Brad Wong, addressed the phenomenon of second-generation racism. He described it as the pain from a racist incident that is passed on to the next generation. The dynamic occurs when a family member experiences racism at work, at church or in the community. Perhaps someone makes a hurtful comment. Or the family member doesn't receive a promotion because his accent makes others think he is ignorant. The person victimized by racism then unwittingly passes on the effects to the next generation. This may come in the form of pressuring children to succeed, expressing destructive anger or inflicting some other reactive response to the racist incident on them.

For some parents who have experienced racism, having their kids succeed validates and justifies the struggles and costliness of immigration. One of the most prominent forms of racism for Asians is the "perpetual foreigner" status. *Where are you from? Why don't you go back to where you came from?* Daily reminders that they don't belong can be refuted when a child is admitted to an elite school, or buys a certain kind of car, or belongs to a certain club. Making it financially or socially in America validates one's right to be here. Sometimes the effects of racism pass unconsciously to the next generation.

My mother came to the United States from Japan as a teenager. Her family of seven lived in a converted garage. They hung their clothes on a line that went across the room and over the giant bed where they all slept. My grandfather was a gardener who worked on the lawns of people up the hill. He would bring home bags of clothing donated by his clients, and my mother and aunties would pick through the clothes for wearable items. My mother never mentioned that she was embarrassed to do this. Nor did she tell me that people made fun of her clothes. But she did tell me, "I was very good at math and wanted to be an emergency-room nurse. But I decided to be a fashion designer because I wanted to wear nice clothes." Reading between the lines, I understand that her experience of wearing other people's clothes affected her career decision. And it affected my sister and me. Every year for Easter, my mother would make us brand-new outfits of fancy lace with matching hats to wear to church. Throughout junior high and high school, my mother designed and sewed most of our party clothes.

Fara grew up in Texas. Perfectionism was her response to racism:

> I went to private schools where I was the only Korean American besides my younger sister. My teachers and my friends had values distinct from my family's values, so I unintentionally assumed that my family was wrong, that they were irrational. I could feel the inherent differences between my school friends and me, but I couldn't pinpoint why those differences existed. I only knew that I looked different, and in junior high and high school, being different is hard. Although there wasn't obvious verbal discrimination or stereotyping toward me, a subtle disregard for my ethnicity or avoidance of who I was left me feeling constantly overlooked. As a result I never felt completely known. I believed that my ethnicity wasn't worth much, that there wasn't anything good about being Korean.

So I would try to make up for that by doing good things, making huge efforts to make friends, thinking that, for people to accept me, I had to be accommodating and nice and assimilate to their ways. I would try to win people's respect with my achievements in school, piano and tennis. So I would throw myself into practicing and studying, thinking that if I excelled in those areas, people would notice me. And it seemed to work! After I won awards in those three areas, everyone knew who I was, and they would say stuff like "Hey, you're the one who's good at tennis."

Like Fara, I decided that I had to be as good as I possibly could. I would read homework instructions several times, just to make sure I was doing exactly what I was supposed to do. I tried to be the perfect kid, perfect student and perfect athlete. I became very quick at figuring out what was expected of me and trying to meet or exceed those expectations.

My kendo sensei told me, "You have to pay special attention to how you dress. The expectations for neatness are higher for women. Make sure your *gi* is tucked in, your knots are even, and all straps are hanging at the same length. Outer appearance reflects inner character." I learned to hide my imperfections—I didn't know if it was safe to go outside and show them. I became very concerned with how my actions looked on the outside.

In reality, my outer appearance didn't truly reflect my inner character; rather, it reflected what people told me I should be—strong, always striving, ambitious, humble, smart, athletic. In a word . . . *perfect.* Inside I was scared to fail. I didn't know if people would like me if I stopped meeting and exceeding their expectations. If I made a mistake, if I insulted someone or made someone uncomfortable, would he think I was a bad person? Or would he think that I just didn't know better? I was too scared to find out. Jesus had some words to say about outer appearances reflecting inner character—but I didn't discover that till much later.

BEYOND THE ASIAN BUBBLE
For a long time, I didn't realize that the expectation for perfect behavior was

Dyadic Culture Versus Individual Culture

Asian culture is a dyadic culture. Like the Jewish culture of Jesus' day, dyadic cultures look outside for a personal definition. What others think of me and tell me to do determines who I am. American culture is an individualistic culture. People are defined internally and encouraged to express who they are inside.

Dyadic and individualistic cultures have good and bad sides. Dyadic cultures can lead to exclusivity and injustice. Others who are outside the norm are excluded, and the peril of any who aren't a part of the group is ignored. A dyadic culture also puts pressure on its members to conform. Individualistic culture can lead to self-absorption. The fulfillment of the self is the highest aim—without regard for what is good for the community. Left on its own, individual culture resists conformity.

cultural. I thought everyone had the same expectations. Yet in my Caucasian friends' homes, their parents uttered exotic phrases like "At least you tried your best." They encouraged them to express themselves. I was shocked as I sat at a dinner table and heard my friend interrupt the conversation and correct her parents. She was given no reprimanding look; the conversation simply continued. In my home, I would never point out my parent's mistake in front of guests.

Then I spent a weekend at the home of Daniela, one of my Latina friends. Sitting around the table, we ate together. Her youngest cousin, about seven, ran to the matriarch's enormous chair. The abuela (grandmother) caressed the face of her little granddaughter. Tucking her into the crook of her arm, she cooed, "Mi cariña" (my beloved). *How beautiful! How smart!*

I was shocked. My grandmother doesn't hug me, let alone use words of endearment. This Latino family broke the rules ingrained in me. Daniela's family welcomed me in. There was no formality. Without asking about what I had done, they enfolded me into their circle.

The expectations for perfection are external. They come from my family, my community, my culture. They are the voices of my family—blood and unrelated. These voices tell me to keep the family business within the family. Mistakes stay within the family; a perfect ideal is presented for others. In kabuki theater, actors use a Noh mask—an expressionless face. Its neutral expression works for every situation. As a child I learned to create a Noh mask, perfect for every situation. To show who I really was might get messy; worse, it could cause shame. My Noh mask created the perfect exterior to cover any imperfections lurking underneath.

RIGHT SCHOOL, RIGHT JOB, RIGHT SPOUSE, WRONG LIFE

When I was in sixth grade, I wrote to Harvard to request an application for college. I didn't really know what college was, but I knew from the stories around the dinner table that if I went, it would be an OK place.

When I expressed an interest in going into theater, quick, sharp comments revealed my lunacy. *Who would hire an Asian actress?* With that dream destroyed, I found a new career during a family vacation to SeaWorld. I wanted to train dolphins and swim with whales. My interest in marine biology was met with stories of the dangers of smelling like fish.

The stories, the fables of my childhood, told me all I needed to know. I decided to be an engineer because of the three acceptable professions of medicine, law and engineering, it fit me best. My cousin in Minnesota had become a doctor. My aunts and uncles worked as lawyers. The older folks around the table spoke of engineering in the same tone. I heard the unspoken words of criticism and judgment loud and clear—any profession other than the three would be unacceptable. I spoke "indirect communication" fluently.

Based on my family's and community's expectations and my own set of standards, I had to strive to choose the right school and right major, be in the right church, have the right looks and behavior, live in the right neighborhood, wear the right clothes, drive the right car, and date and marry someone of the right ethnicity.

Refined over generations, the collective wisdom appears to offer guidelines for guaranteed success. As a dyadic culture, the group determines the actions of the individual. The enormous expectations for success set up most people for failure—after all, only one person in a class can be a valedictorian. Unrealistic standards serve only to increase the striving for perfectionism.

As a woman, I have perfectionist tendencies. Then my Japanese culture adds a communal dynamic that reinforces the need for perfect behavior. My understanding of Christianity added yet another "perfection" obligation. The weight of the three "perfects" created an impossible load.

For a while I struggled to try to achieve these ideals—I wanted to be perfect for God, for my family and for myself. But after a while, I found myself failing. So I settled with appearing perfect on the outside. The strain of trying to meet so many expectations was tiring. Before I discovered God's redemption of my perfectionist tendencies, before I heard his invitation to be transformed, I fell for a lot of lies. It took awhile for me to see that God was *perfecting* me, not expecting me to be perfect. It was about his work in me, not my work for him. In many ways, I had believed the promises of perfection more than I believed God's promises.

I imported this value for perfection unknowingly into my discipleship. "Be perfect, therefore, as your heavenly Father is perfect" (Mt 5:48). Perfection took on a new and scary spiritualized form: *God will love me if I do things right*. So on the outside, I tried to play the part of the perfect Christian—go to the right church, have the right Bible, be an active member in my fellowship, go to the right conferences. But my insides didn't necessarily match what was going on outside. I made mistakes, but I covered them behind the perfect, placid, always happy Christian exterior. It was my Christian Noh mask. The freedom God promised had no meaning for me. I felt trapped by a demanding God, in the same way that I felt trapped by the perfectionist demands of my community, my family and myself.

Not surprisingly, my perfectionism created barriers in my relationship with God. I had trouble receiving God's love—I could focus only on myself and my flaws. I thought, *He would never love me—look what I've done.* I focused on my actions rather than God's power, and as a result he became powerless in my mind. With my strong performance mentality, I came to assume that I could earn God's favor and blessings. I reduced him to a bribable God. He came under my control.

Ultimately, all this created a tremendous amount of pride. I thought that I had the ability to do things perfectly and that God should reward me with a good life if I did what I was supposed to do. Perfectionism drove me deep into myself and away from God.

But I was scared. My life was broken. I was doing wrong all the time. I just wouldn't admit it to myself. I had no category for flaws. If I do something wrong, *I* must *be* wrong.

In college I was sleeping with my boyfriend. At the same time, I was really involved in a Christian fellowship. People told me they respected me for my Christian faith. But I felt unknown by them. I had created a perfect front—they were interacting with that, not with the real me. Would they still like me if they knew the truth? As my inner world dissolved, I worked harder to hold up the perfect front. I was scared others would find out just how bad my life was.

I would dodge questions about my boyfriend and quickly change the subject. I avoided asking my friends questions about their relationships—even when they asked me to keep them accountable. I didn't want the questions to come back to me. Sometimes people would ask me directly, "So how is the physical aspect of your relationship?" My answers came back vague—"Oh, it's OK. We struggle with physical boundaries, but I think that things are really improving." I spoke in generalities and used deceptive words that had double meanings—I hoped others would assume the best. I deluded myself: *I'm not lying, just not telling the full truth.* But I was purposefully misleading my friends. I was lying to them and to myself.

I couldn't live and be honest about what I was doing. So instead I rationalized our behavior—*We really care about each other. This is just a physical act that represents our emotional intimacy. I'm sure we're going to get married. I* couldn't be honest with myself because I had no category for being a flawed person. And this was a huge flaw. It was quickly turning from a flaw into a major character issue.

I even thought I could hide the bad stuff from God. Would he still like me if he knew? I wasn't sure he would. It was a scary loop. The freedom God promised had no meaning for me.

Finally things got really bad. Lying to my Christian community, my friends, my family and myself was too much to keep up. During a short missions project in San Francisco, I asked the director if I could say something to the group. Right after worship, I stood up and confessed everything—unprompted, unsolicited. I needed to unload and be real with everyone. It was terrifying, and I wasn't sure how people would respond. They took it very seriously: living a hidden life is a dangerous habit.

That confession began a process for me.

My response to the temptation to sleep with my boyfriend was to try harder, work harder to keep this from happening. It revealed my picture of a perfect and demanding God who demands perfection from me and leaves me on my own to accomplish his perfect and unattainable will.

But then God invited me to take off the Noh mask. I was both justified and a sinner. I had thought I was one or the other. Could I take off my mask and live transparently in the tension between being a sinner and being justified?

I decided to seek out people with flaws whom God loved. Maybe by understanding their stories I would discover freedom. Perhaps I could come out from behind the mask. God invited me. But could I?

Hero or Bad Guy?

My search for flawed characters lead me to David. King David was a hero in my church. If David had grown up in my community, the Lakeside church ladies would have whispered his accomplishments. *Ah, he's the smallest and the youngest, so humble but so favored.* David believed in God's power over Goliath's. He stood for God. He was a man after God's own heart. David set another unattainable standard of perfection.

Or did he? God sought out David, a humble runt of the family litter, when King Saul strayed. He elevated David to a place of honor. David went on to write most of the psalms. David was a man to be emulated.

But David was also a thief, a liar, a murderer, an adulterer, a man of many wives and concubines, who possessed women at his whim and fancy. He was so violent that God wouldn't allow him to build the temple. David's crimes put him in the top ten of the bad boys of the Bible. Most of the Pharisees led more pure and perfect lives than he did.

And yet God called him a man after his own heart. Why? It wasn't because he was perfect or even because he was mostly good. He failed the test of perfection. He failed the moral test of excellence. He failed often. But it's not about David and what he did right or wrong. It's about God and who God is.

I used to think that God wanted me to be perfect. After failing in my Christian life, I stopped striving for perfection. It was unattainable. But David's example began to rewrite my view of failure. He made a lot of public mistakes, and they are recorded in the Bible for generations to read. But the story of David is not a "how-to" manual for finding favor with God. The story of David is not about David. It's about God and how he views David. It's the story of God's great love and faithfulness to a violent, sinful man— the story of how God shows favor though David cannot do anything to earn it. God does this because that is who he is.

In God's response to David, I began to see a little more of God's true character. He never called us to perfect ourselves. I had taken "be perfect" in Matthew 5:48 as "do nothing wrong." I had taken the verse to mean, "Do the right things. Don't make a mistake." I thought that perfection was even a prerequisite for God's love. But a truer meaning of *perfect* is "complete, lacking in nothing, fulfilled, whole because of Christ." And I began to see that while God longs for our perfection, he doesn't require it of us. God is in the process of perfecting us, just as he loved David during, through and after all of his many failures.

God called me to see myself as his daughter, already redeemed, already sanctified, precious in his sight. Isaiah 43:4 says, "You are precious in my sight, and honored, and I love you." God says this to Israel, a nation of broken and unfaithful people. People like me.

Precious? How could I be precious? I've made so many mistakes.

When I make a mistake, I quickly remember everything I've done wrong, and I begin to spiral downward. Do I believe the message of being precious, over and above the demands and false promises of perfectionism? I can only acknowledge my mistake while holding on to God's promises in the face of my own mistakes.

In repeating his promise, I began to sense a different call from God. He calls me to be faithful in the moment. He does not load up my daily to-do list with more than I can do, and then shake his head when I fail to overperform his expectations.

I had seen God as being like a mother who disdains the macaroni necklace that her child made for her. She looks at it and thinks: *This will never match anything I have; she should have made me a blue one.* She accepts the macaroni necklace with an "I know you did your best" sigh of sadness. If God is like this, I fail him, every day.

But I began to understand that God is like a mother who enjoys her child's gift. Instead of criticizing, she coos over the sloppy string of macaroni, covered in clashing colors. She delights in the colors and the gift because she loves her child. That is our God.

I bought into the myth that God loved me for what I could do. But that's a lie. It's a scary and secretly prideful lie, because believing that what I do, how perfect I am, determines how lovable I am, puts me at the top. It is all about me and how I can earn God's love. It's about my self-sufficiency and how my actions alone can earn God's approval. As God made clear to David, his love is not about me and my performance. It's about my God who created, delights in and loves me, regardless of what I do and what ideals I have attained or how close to perfect I am in my own eyes. And it is about his power, which is made perfect in weaknesses (1 Cor 12:9).

I fail often—the lustful thought I can't get out of my mind, the quickness of my anger. My jealousy of others bubbles just below my ability to keep it in check. I lie, spin the truth, avoid taking responsibility for what I do wrong. Perfectionism leads me to deflect because it gives me no category for making a mistake.

But then I see the parent who receives the child's sloppy macaroni necklace. She receives with delight—she has no expectation of a masterpiece. My view of myself has shifted from a frustrated striver to a child: *Who am I to create a masterpiece? I'm just a kid.*

God calls me to live in the reality of being precious and honored—in my dating relationships, my family, my work, my church. He does not call me to perfection. He calls me to transformation. And transformation requires putting aside the mask that creates a false perfect exterior. This means acknowledging my need for help and for change and admitting that I am not able to do it. It involves confessing to God and others. It involves inviting him into the places in me that are broken. It means breaking from habits of self-sufficiency and moving toward dependence on God. It means trusting in God's perfecting process rather than working toward my idea of perfection.

God longs to transform and redeem the expectations we import from our culture. Transformation has meant rejecting some of the false perfectionism of my Asian culture. I sometimes feel like a failure because I don't follow the traditional script for Asian American women. I feel a subtle and daily rejection from the Asian community because I am in full-time ministry. I'm not doing what I'm supposed to be doing. I carry a burden because I've left a path of guaranteed respect, security, my parents' happiness. Instead I've chosen a deviant path. On my worst days, I feel like a disappointment. On my best days, I feel like a prophet, stretching the boundaries of "things that Asian women do." Embracing God's acceptance of me has helped me put into perspective (and put to rest) some of the false expectations in my culture.

By the time I was in college, I had become tired of striving for and perpetually missing perfection. God was good enough to show me that I cannot reach it, nor does he require it of me. This began a shift in me, a shift that isn't done yet. Slowly, God's words are beginning to sink in—I'm changing from one who needs to perform for the pleasure of her God to one who knows she is loved by her God. My prayers have changed from asking God, "What do you want me to do?" to "Who do you hope I will become?"

I am learning to receive less-than-perfect conditions as a part of life and not as obstacles to overcome. I'm growing in acceptance of my lack of perfection. A couple of practices have helped me become more comfortable with imperfection. I try to remember that God does not expect perfection of me; rather, he's transforming and in the process of perfecting me. Realizing that I'm in a process helps me feel OK with making mistakes. I've tried to be better about admitting my mistakes and telling others. Admitting my mistakes and confessing takes practice, but I have found it to be liberating.

My father, unlike some fathers in the Chinese families I grew up with, treated me and my brothers equally. So I didn't have any problems thinking that I, as a girl, was as good and capable as my brothers. However, I learned that "one must not make mistakes, because one must try to do everything perfectly all the time." (I found this in a letter that my dad wrote me when my younger brother and I were in kindergarten and grade two. Dad learned from my mom that I had made some mistakes in my homework.)

By the time I began working with my friend Geri, it was pretty ingrained in me that making mistakes is shameful. But God used Geri's and my friendship to develop me as a Christian leader. Geri affirms my leadership often by recommending me as a biblical teacher, speaker or trainer in different settings. I have deeply appreciated the times when she helped me to believe that "failure is not the last word" and pushed me to risk things that I might not otherwise do, because I might not do it well.

DONNA DONG,
DIRECTOR OF MULTIETHNIC MINISTRY,
INTERVARSITY CANADA

When things are not going well, I try to say, "Everything is as perfect as it can be." This redefines perfection for me. It helps me to embrace the wrinkles of each day as part of the fabric of life. Other times, when I'm focusing on flaws, I try to practice the discipline of gratitude. I thank God for all the things that *are* going well. I thank him for even the small things—a roof, a bed, a hot meal, friends—and this returns my focus to him and away from my (or others') flaws.

It helps to hear others tell their own stories of failure. They teach me more about character and courage than success stories do. Asking people I respect, "What's the biggest mistake you made and what did you learn from it?" has taught me a lot. Talking about mistakes with people I admire has helped me to realize that it's a part of every story. And being open about my mistakes, not just my successes, with others lets God's power shine more clearly.

It's good to get comfortable even in the midst of failing. A couple of years ago, I decided to take jazz singing classes. I've never been a good singer, but I've always enjoyed jazz. And I thought it would be good for me to try learning a new skill, especially since I wasn't sure that I could do it. It was scary being a beginner. But the freedom to experiment, fail and learn was so liberating. Being in a new place, without my props of success, made me feel vulnerable, but I learned to stop striving and instead to just enjoy the experience.

I'm learning to be comfortable with failing every day. My everyday failures lead me to God's words of sufficiency. The words of love affirm that I am whole and not defined by my failures or my attempts at perfection. Instead of seeing temptations and brokenness as obstacles between God and me, I begin to see them as opportunities that push me into deeper relationship with him and with others. Weakness leads me to depend on God, even as I try to not listen to the lies that drove me toward perfectionism. I used to believe that God would love me more; I used to believe that life had a specific path for success that I had to follow; I used to believe that I could work really hard and create my own happiness.

All these drove me toward perfectionism. But now it is in the midst of my flaws, and not in spite of them, that I find God's love. When the power of appearing flawless to others was broken, the bonds of perfectionism were broken. Finding that my parents and friends still loved me even when I made mistakes helped me to understand God's unconditional love.

God redefined flaws and failures in my life. From perfectionism to faithfulness, from failure to transformation: God rewrites and redeems our culture's expectations.

As I broke free from perfectionism, I hated my culture and all its impossible expectations. But then God began to redeem my perfectionism. He recycled tools of my perfectionism to use for his kingdom—a vision for excellence, the ability to accept delayed gratification, attention to detail, commitment and thorough execution.

Perfectionism redeemed has amazing implications for the kingdom of God. Performance orientation, a byproduct of perfectionism, can be redeemed. I've seen groups of Asians create amazing presentations, projects and performances. Some students at UC Berkeley once put on a celebration of Christian artists. They communicated the gospel through spoken word, dance and drama. It was a compelling evening, full of new and amazing insights about God. Collective vision and skillful execution can unleash startling creativity for communicating the gospel in new and compelling ways. I'm awed at the creative potential within my community—for evangelism, worship and justice.

The wrinkle in my sister's dress lives only in my mother's memory and mine. A mechanical failure destroyed all the professional photos of the ceremony. The photographer had no proofs to show. I force myself to remember the good parts of that amazing and sacred day—the look of my sister as she entered the sanctuary, a private smile, my mother crying in the front row. With gratitude, I treasure every moment I do remember.

perfection
try harder
do better
not quite
sufficient
exceeding
beyond
becoming

4

From Swallowing Suffering

T R A C E Y G E E

They all were taught to desire nothing,

to swallow other people's misery,

to eat their own bitterness.

A M Y T A N , *T H E J O Y L U C K C L U B*

A few years ago, I went to a women's weekend retreat with my church. We gathered in a small hotel outside of L.A. On the first morning, we had an open testimony time. As the sharing was winding down, Lily Tatsuno got up to speak. About eighty years old, she navigated her walker through the rows of chairs and finally reached the microphone. She had just lost her husband to cancer that year, she told us; further, she had battled cancer herself twice before and was now battling it once again. Yet Lily glowed with peaceful joy. She said, "Jesus has never let me down my whole life long, and I believe he's good to me."

After that, we decorated cookies, worshiped, met in small groups and heard from a great speaker. But it was Lily's words that made the biggest impression on me. How could she speak of her husband's death and her repeated battles with cancer and yet talk about how Jesus is good in the same breath? Her whole being radiated faith. Not long after that conference Lily went home to be with the Lord, but her words left an indelible impression on me. I decided, *I want to be like Lily when I grow up.*

In 2 Corinthians 11:23-32, the apostle Paul lists the sufferings he's been through—beatings, shipwrecks and other hardships. Some of these trials, like sleepless nights, seem small. Some are a lot bigger—for example, being stoned. It's quite an extensive list.

If an Asian American woman were writing 2 Corinthians 11, the chapter might be a lot shorter, because we might not dare to make a list like that. We might not think our struggles and pain qualify as bona fide suffering since so many people are going through things that are much worse. We might think that our past sufferings are better left untouched, unspoken. We might not want to admit that we currently are in the midst of painful situations or relationships.

But the truth is, we all have our own list. We have all had to go through suffering on some level. What makes some people end up bitter, resentful or hopeless and others end up like Lily?

WHY DO WE SUFFER?

Sometimes we suffer because of bad choices we've made, but that's not the only reason. Sometimes we suffer because we feel helpless to try to change things that we desperately wish could be different. Sometimes we suffer because we have been disappointed—things didn't turn out the way we wanted. We have to deal with sickness, death, broken relationships and injustice. These things were not part of God's original design for his creation. Often when we experience pain we wonder if we are being punished for some mistake we made. However, a lot of the pain we go through is because of the fact that we live in a fallen and broken world. We wish we could avoid it, but many times we can't.

The Asian worldview takes suffering for granted. In his book *Invitation to Lead,* Paul Tokunaga highlights some of the major threads of suffering throughout the histories of Asian countries: colonialism and civil unrest in

India, Pakistan, Bangladesh and Sri Lanka; death and suffering in Cambodia and Vietnam; the *han* of Korea's history; the bombing of Hiroshima and Nagasaki in Japan; the rape of Nanking in China; the internment of Japanese Americans during World War II. "Clearly Asian history is laced with episodic suffering. But unlike the Western disposition toward it (suffering is abnormal, an aberration) Asians live with their histories blended with belief systems that see suffering as normative and expected."[1]

In the Asian worldview, suffering is simply an assumed part of the way the world is. Sickness, disease and famine are accepted as natural parts of life. In contrast, the American worldview sees suffering as an abnormal state. A friend of mine once remarked that, when suffering happens, Americans ask God to take the suffering away; when people in other parts of the world suffer, they ask God for strength to endure it well.

Asian Americans are caught between those two ways of understanding suffering. Our Asian heritage can bring a corrective to the view that suffering is unusual or strange. The New Testament writers don't ask why suffering and pain exist. They assume that they are part of living in a world that is fallen. The writers focus on an eternal perspective. On the other hand, we do not want to fall into the fatalism that can accompany Asian thinking about suffering. *Well, there's nothing I can do about it. Life is going to be hard and painful, so I guess I just have to brace myself and get through it.*

Sometimes we suffer because of the gospel. Jesus never promised that following him guarantees a suffering-free life. He used phrases like "when you suffer," not "if you suffer." He taught his disciples how to endure suffering, not how to avoid it. If we try to pursue a life without suffering, we won't get very far. All evidence points to the fact that suffering is unavoidable.

Try to imagine a life in which you never experienced heartache, sadness, pain or suffering of any kind. Try to imagine the effort it would take to constantly protect yourself and control the uncontrollable. Think about the emotional distance you would need to maintain in order to never get close enough to another person to be hurt by them. It doesn't sound possible, it doesn't sound like a good way to live, but most of us unconsciously try to do just that.

Realizing that suffering is inevitable, however, points us in a completely different direction. If that is true, the most important question isn't *How can I avoid suffering?* but *How can I handle suffering well? How can I experience suffering with God's grace, presence and redemption?* These questions can change the whole course of a person's life. They can determine whether you have a life of resentment, anger and hopelessness or a life of character, endurance and hope.

In the Middle of the Storm

Last year my father was diagnosed with cancer. I was washing the dinner dishes one night when my mother called, sobbing, to tell me the news. In shock, I slumped down on the kitchen floor and tried to ask questions. My voice was suddenly small and scared. I felt as if my whole world changed with that phone call.

During the months when my father was undergoing chemotherapy and radiation treatment, I was tired and emotionally drained. I had very little to give to others. My husband and my good friends came around me to offer support, encouragement and prayers, but all their love couldn't make the pain go away. Some days I felt hopeful. Other days I felt scared and alone.

I often felt guilty. I lacked energy to do things that I usually loved doing. I had very little energy for my work. Some people had no idea what was going on in my life, so they treated me as if all was normal. But I was constantly aware of what my dad and my family were going through.

Some people who knew about my father just didn't know what to say. I work with college students; many of them had not had to deal with sickness and death and couldn't understand what I was experiencing. At times I felt alone. As I watched my dad lose forty pounds, struggle with the treatment, and go in and out of the hospital, I felt helpless. And always I felt sad. At random moments—in the grocery store or after seeing a sentimental commercial on TV—I felt like bursting into tears.

When it was announced that my dad was cancer free, in remission, suddenly I could breathe again.

Looking back on those months, I realize that it is really hard to know how to deal with suffering. Most of the time, we want to escape and will try to find some way to make the pain stop. In this case, that was not possible. There was nothing I could do to make my dad well. It's so hard to know what to do with pain, anger and questions. *Why is this happening? Where are you, God? I don't know if I can get through this.* Women get a lot of advice on what clothes and makeup to wear; we do not get very much to help us learn how to deal with suffering well.

SWALLOWING SORROW

Growing up, I learned that there is nowhere for suffering to go, so all you can do is swallow it. I remember standing in our kitchen talking to my seventy-two-year-old grandma after my mom had been diagnosed with cancer. I had never before seen her cry, and with my limited fourth-grade Chinese vocabulary I couldn't find the words to comfort her. She told me that my mom was sick because she had swallowed her sorrow. That was her explanation of what was happening to my mom: not cancer cells or carcinogens or diet and exercise—the problem was that she had swallowed her suffering.

Going to God in suffering is easier said than done. We Asian American women tend to swallow our sorrow, pretending it's not there. *It's not that bad. I'm fine. I shouldn't complain. Other people have to go through worse, so I should be thankful. Maybe I did something to deserve this—I brought it on myself.*

We find it hard to be honest with others. We don't want to be a burden. Perhaps this is linked to the cultural value of saving face. We mistakenly think that it is shameful to admit our struggles or to own up to "negative" emotions like pain, sadness and anger. It's not OK to feel those things, so we try to pretend they are not there.

Maybe it's even harder to be honest with God. It's hard to talk to him about our real doubt and anger. But when we avoid honesty and swallow our sorrow, we cut ourselves off from him. "Perhaps our relationship with God is like our relationship with anyone else we care about: If we are not honest with the other person concerning our feelings, desires, and needs, then the relationship withers and perhaps it dies."[2]

It is hard to deal with our emotions. We may know that God is good in our heads or when everything is going well. But periods of suffering press all our emotions to the edge. Our hearts may not be caught up with our heads. Unfortunately, Christians sometimes offer trite catch phrases that don't help: *If you believe enough, you won't feel bad. Everything happens for a reason.* While these slogans may have a grain of truth, when we are suffering it is hard to hear simplistic answers.

But we don't have to just swallow our sorrow. Jesus offers us more than simplistic answers or swallowing our sorrow.

MARY, MARTHA AND LAZARUS

Several years ago I was dealing with a difficult situation. There was a financial crisis in my family. I doubted God really cared. I felt helpless to change anything. Money seemed like the answer to all my problems, and I found myself putting all my hope in it. But amid my pain and confusion, my friend Kevin pointed me to chapters 11 and 12 of John to help me see where God was in the midst of my struggles. That passage became the main way I stayed connected to God through that difficult time.

Mary and Martha have a brother named Lazarus, who is very sick. John tells us that Jesus knows and loves this family. The sisters send a message to Jesus to hurry because they are so concerned about Lazarus's failing health. Then the worst-case scenario happens: Lazarus dies before Jesus gets there. By the time Jesus finally arrives, Lazarus has been dead for four days.

The two sisters react very differently. Martha hears that Jesus is coming and hurries to greet him. She's willing to go to him even though she is upset. She tells him, "If you had been here, my brother would not have died" (11:21). You can hear the pain in her voice as she bluntly expresses her suffering. But she also expresses her hope; Martha knows that Jesus has what she needs. She adds, "But I know that even now God will give you whatever you ask" (11:22).

Mary responds differently. She does not come out to greet Jesus. Has she not heard that Jesus is coming? I think she is so distraught that she can't even go out to meet him. Maybe she is angry with him, wishing he had shown up and prevented the death in the first place. She stays in the house, away from Jesus.

The day we talked, my friend Kevin saw me as Mary. I was hurting, but I was staying in the house away from Jesus, and his exhortation to me was "Don't stay in the house. Come out and interact with Jesus."

It seems so simple—come out of the house and interact with Jesus in your suffering. But at the time it felt so hard. I didn't feel able to come to Jesus, because I didn't know if he cared about the things that were so painful to me. I felt angry at him, so I wanted to ignore him. But doing that stifled me emotionally and spiritually.

FROM SUFFERING TO REDEMPTION

Mary's story helps us see how we can bring our suffering to Jesus rather than swallowing it. Her journey goes through five stages, and each part is important. In our lives, a stage can blend into the next, or the order may vary. One stage is not a prerequisite to another. Still, Mary's journey can help show us how to experience Jesus when we're going through painful times.

Avoidance: Staying in the house, away from Jesus. At first, Mary stays in the house and isn't willing to come out to him. Many times we get stuck in the house, away from Jesus. We aren't willing to come to him because we don't think he cares, or we're angry, or we're just trying to avoid our feelings. But if we stay here, we become isolated from people and from God. Sometimes we need someone to call us to come out, as Martha did for Mary. That's what my friend Kevin did. He recognized how important it was for me to get out of the house and called me to at least get up and interact with Jesus about how I felt.

Telling the truth: Speaking honestly with Jesus. Mary finally takes the important step of coming out of the house. She says the same thing that Martha did: "Lord, if you had been here, my brother would not have died." She's basically saying, "Where were you when I needed you, Jesus? I thought you cared. This is the worst thing that could have happened. I don't understand why you didn't come." She is honest with him. She pours out her pain and what she is really feeling. She doesn't swallow it and pretend that she understands when she doesn't. She doesn't cover up her true pain, feelings and questions. She knows that she can be honest with Jesus.

Sometimes we think that being a "good Christian" means that we never tell Jesus anything negative. We feel as if we can't say anything to him that isn't happy or joyful because then we'd be saying he's not good. We're not supposed to feel anger and confusion and hurt, so we don't express them to God. That is part of swallowing our sorrow. But we see Mary bringing her pain to Jesus. Her journey doesn't end here, but this is such an important step.

"As a father has compassion for his children, so the LORD has compassion for those who fear him. For he knows how we were made; he remembers that we are dust" (Ps 103:13-14). God remembers that we are fragile. God is like a father who has compassion for his children.

Recently I was talking to my friend as he played with his daughter. She's about a year and a half old, and she was exploring the arm of the couch. When she fell and bumped her head, she started crying. Her dad immediately picked her up, held her and comforted her. He didn't tell her to deal with it on her own. He didn't tell her to get over it. He didn't ignore her cries. He immediately went to her and comforted her. The psalmist says God is that kind of father.

God knows that we are creatures who are subject to suffering and pain. He doesn't ask us to be stronger than we are. He doesn't need us to swallow pain or pretend that we are always happy. He can handle our honest emotions, our pain and our questions. In fact, the psalms are filled with voices of people who are in pain and crying out to God. When Lazarus died, Jesus heard Martha and Mary's emotions, pain and questions. He can hear ours too.

Experiencing Jesus' compassion. When Mary pours out her suffering, Jesus doesn't tell her that she's making too much of it. He doesn't tell her to stop complaining. He doesn't compare her suffering to anyone else's. And he doesn't minimize what she's feeling. Instead he weeps with her. John 11:33

says, "When Jesus saw her weeping, and the Jews who came with her also weeping, he was greatly disturbed in spirit and deeply moved."

Sometimes we imagine Jesus being far away from our suffering. Sometimes we imagine him being frustrated with us and telling us to get over it. Sometimes we imagine him as stoic and unmoved. That notion of God comes from ancient Greek philosophy; it is not the Bible's understanding of God. Here we see Jesus having compassion to the point of tears. When he sees Mary in the midst of one of the hardest things she will ever have to experience, he is moved. He is deeply compassionate, involved and close to us in our grief. That is who Jesus is to us. He is gentle and tender with the brokenhearted.

Experiencing Jesus' redemption. Mary has experienced her worst fear: her brother has died. But then she also sees the miracle of Jesus' raising Lazarus from the dead. But she has to wait for it.

Maybe four days doesn't seem like that much to you. Maybe you've had to wait a lot longer than four days for Jesus' redemption. But the point is that Mary had to wait a lot longer than she wanted. She wanted Jesus to come before Lazarus died, and it wasn't in her plan that he would show up after her brother had been in the tomb for four days. It wasn't as she expected or as quickly as she wanted. It wasn't in her timing. But Jesus came through for her.

We may need to wait for Jesus' redemption. It may take a lot longer than we expected. It may not happen according to our timing. But Jesus' redemption will come.

When I started to open up to God with my feelings about my dad's cancer, answers did not come right away. There were many days when I didn't hear anything from God, but I just had to continue to pursue him. I remember Christmas that year—marked by trips to the emergency room, sitting in hospital waiting rooms, my dad's treatments, how the chemo affected him, how sick he was. It didn't seem as if God was giving many answers at the time. I needed to learn to continue to wait.

"And we know that God causes all things to work together for good to those who love God, to those who are called according to His purpose"

(Rom 8:28 NASB). God will intervene. He gets involved in our lives—in *all things,* including all the suffering. Romans says that God brings good and redemption in any and all circumstances we ever have or will face. It's not just hopeful optimism. Based on his character, we have hope. We have hope in God, the compassionate and powerful God of all creation, who rights wrongs and confronts injustice, who is at work to bring comfort and restore our broken world.

> Jesus may not give the kind of victory we expect. But he will always overcome trouble in some way if we ask him. His answer in trying circumstances may be relief; but it may equally be endurance. His answer in illness may be health; but it may be courage instead. He may plan rescue from death's door, or permit bereavement and give new hope with it. But "in all these things we are more than conquerors through him who loved us" (Rom 8:37).[3]

Whenever we come to Jesus and ask him for his help and power in our suffering, he will come through for us.

Deep love and intimacy with Jesus. "Mary took a pound of costly perfume made of pure nard, anointed Jesus' feet, and wiped them with her hair. The house was filled with the fragrance of the perfume" (John 12:3). In the end, Mary has a heart so full of love and gratitude for Jesus that she can't help but let it spill out as she anoints his feet with costly perfume.

This is the kind of relationship with Jesus that I want to have. I want to pour out the costly perfume of my life at Jesus' feet. I want this kind of love for Jesus and intimacy with him. I want this kind of freedom with him. But I can't have that unless I come to him with my sorrow. Mary could not have gotten to this point without coming out of the house. I can't have this kind of relationship with Jesus if I swallow my sorrow. I need to bring it to him and interact with him over it if I am going to have deep intimacy with and love for Jesus.

THE CRUCIAL STEP

It was crucial for Mary to come out of the house and tell Jesus the honest truth of what she was feeling. Too often we get hung up and stay inside. It's easy to stay there. But if Mary had stayed in that place in avoidance, she wouldn't have experienced all that Jesus had to offer her. We cannot let ourselves stay in the house and swallow our sorrow. Jesus is waiting for us to come out.

Mary became my model, and reading her story helped me to remember my friend's exhortation to come out of the house. And I also discovered small steps I could take to bring myself to Jesus in periods of suffering:

- The Psalms have helped me learn how to bring questions and anger to God in the midst of suffering. Reading psalms in times of suffering helps me open up to God about my emotions and questions. I read them aloud as prayers to God.

- It helped to tell Jesus what my unanswered questions were. *Do you really care about my family? What are you doing? Are you here at all?* Most times the answers didn't come quickly. But it helped me to acknowledge that there were unanswered questions connected to a lot of pain. Sometimes that was all I was able to do as prayer.

- It also helped to talk to friends who cared about me and especially friends who had gone through similar struggles. Often I felt like I was being a burden. Surely they didn't have time to talk to me and hear about my problems. But this was an important way for me to not swallow my suffering. I felt as if I was interacting with Jesus and experiencing his care through them.

Other people I know journal, write letters to God or scream if it helps them. The point is that we can't stay in the house. As we take steps toward Jesus, he will meet us and help us to experience his compassion, his redemption and a deeper relationship with him than we've ever had before.

FROM REDEMPTION TO COMPASSION

There is an amazing surprise that comes from this. When we are like Mary and become willing to bring our suffering to Jesus, we gain a profound gift to offer to others. "Blessed be the God and Father of our Lord Jesus Christ, the Father of mercies and the God of all consolation, who consoles us in all our affliction, so that we may be able to console those who are in any affliction with the consolation with which we ourselves are consoled by God" (2 Cor 1:3).

When we experience God's comfort in our suffering, we are able to comfort others who are suffering as well. Second Corinthians says that we offer them God's own comfort. Other people will experience God's comfort through us because we have experienced it ourselves.

My friend Sandy is one of the people God sent to me to get through the time of my father's cancer. More than ten years earlier, her dad had suffered from cancer and had passed away. Sandy had been like Mary—she had brought her suffering to Jesus and experienced redemption. She offered to talk with me and pray for me. It was a turning point when I first talked to her about how I was feeling.

Sandy told me how she felt when her dad was sick—what she went through, what happened and how she handled it. I felt less alone as I listened to her. She gave me something that none of my other friends and family were able to give me, as much as they loved and supported me. She gave me perspective, wisdom, comfort and the assurance that Jesus could bring me through this dark valley. She showed me that it is possible to endure your worst nightmare and come out on the other side of it with Jesus.

Sandy showed me that when we go through suffering and do it with Jesus, we have a tremendous gift to give. We can bring the comfort of God to someone else. It is a gift that we won't have unless we have experienced it with Jesus ourselves. When we choose to let Jesus into our suffering, we are transformed into agents of his comfort for others.

In a world where people are hurting, God sends us out as agents of his love and presence. But we cannot be his agents if we have not allowed God into our own places of suffering.

THE END IS IN SIGHT

Suffering is inevitable. That's the bad news. The good news is that God can do more right in the midst of our suffering than we ever knew—if we let him into it. He has more for us than swallowing our sorrow. He has more for us than trying to escape it. We have a deeply compassionate and loving God who is near to us when we suffer. We have a God who can handle our raw moments of honest despair and who weeps with those who are weeping. We have a God who can redeem suffering even when we can't always see how or when. And we have a God who can make us agents of comfort and blessing for others who are suffering as well.

My husband and I are going though a hard time with our home. Last April, we purchased a condo. It was our first home, and we were so excited. Two months later there was a fire. Nobody got hurt, but our home was left uninhabitable. A year later the necessary repairs have yet to be done because of various complications. All this time, we haven't been able to live at home. It has tried our patience and stretched us in many ways.

At first we were just shocked. I thought this kind of thing happened only on TV. Now we have to deal with it daily. Sometimes we would rather not think about it, but that's not always possible. Because word about the problem has gotten around; about once a week I have a conversation that goes like this:

"So how's your house situation?"

"Not good."

"When do you get to move back in?"

"We don't know."

"Wow, it's taking a long time, isn't it?"

"Yes, it is."

How long has it been?"

"A really long time."

It becomes a little tedious to repeat these depressing facts over and over. But even so, each time I am pressed to keep the end in sight.

We don't know exactly when everything will be done and when we will be able to move back into our home. But we do know that the insurance companies have a contract with us and are bound to take care of the

IN THE VALLEY OF THE SHADOW

During my first year of marriage, my father was diagnosed with terminal lung cancer. In one phone call my world came crashing down as I heard that my father had about six months to live. The next several months were filled with multiple doctors' appointments in which I took the lead, since I had to translate between the doctors and my parents.

About three months after his diagnosis, I was taking care of my dad with my husband while my mom was out doing errands. Dad started having a difficult time breathing, so we called the doctor and decided to take him to the emergency room. As we were driving, I could tell that something was wrong, and I yelled at Doug to drive faster. Just as we pulled off the freeway and were minutes from the hospital, my dad collapsed in my arms and died. They tried to resuscitate him when we arrived at the emergency room, but it was too late.

That began my journey of intense mourning. I was quite literally wandering in "the valley of the shadow of death." During the first year, I cried every day, multiple times a day, feeling as if I was barely functioning. At the end of the year someone told me that she felt let down because I wasn't there for her. I often had to leave during worship times, because I would start to weep. I was clinically depressed, and I was angry at God. But though I was angry at God, I always knew I wasn't going to turn my back on him. I knew I needed him. I knew in my head that he loved me and was committed to me. But I was still angry. I continued on the journey of mourning, which amounted to many wrestling matches with God, for about five years.

That night and for many days, months and some years, I felt devastated. I was in so much pain, I didn't know what to do but just lie there and cry. In my head I knew God was with me all along, especially the night of my dad's death, but in the midst of my pain, devastation, depression and anger, I could not feel his presence.

Over those next five years, I took life a little slower. My supervisors cut down some of my work responsibilities. I saw a counselor. During my prayer times I sometimes sat silently, not because I was practicing silence but because I was so depressed and didn't have anything to say.

Two things helped me during that time. One was that I cried when I needed to cry. I couldn't hide my emotions the way I could before, because the feelings were so strong. I let myself mourn. Second, I was honest with God. I told God how I felt when I was sad, when I was hopeless, when I was angry. At times I vented my anger about my dad's death.

After five years of mourning, I realized that I felt more solid in my faith and in my relationship with God than I had before my dad's sickness. I was more confident about God's love for me and more peaceful about life. As I looked back, I realized that it had helped a lot to mourn and be honest with God. The fact that God walked with me and was not shocked or angry at me for struggling so much gave me a new kind of peace and confidence that I'd ever experienced before.

Since that five-year mark, after I had finally come out of depression, God has brought me many people whose parents have been diagnosed with cancer or whose parents have died. God has redeemed my suffering and has used it for good. It doesn't lessen my pain, but I am encouraged to see my experience of suffering be used to love others.

It's now been twelve years since my dad died. I trust that God was with me that awful night, even though I didn't feel his presence. And I continue to have more experiences of his comfort as I still mourn.

SANDY LEE SCHAUPP

situation. We don't know when, but we do know that *it will happen*. And on that day the house is finished, there will be new carpet and fresh paint, and the place will look even better than it did before.

I can imagine what it will feel like to be able to live in our home again and to invite our friends over to celebrate. We have a picture of what it will look like when it's all over. Amid my frustration and impatience, that picture gives me hope. I know that no matter how bad it looks, it won't be like this forever. Knowing that helps me hang in there.

It's like that with the kingdom of God. We don't know exactly how it will all work out, but we are already promised that we haven't been left as orphans and that someday Jesus will come back and all suffering will end. As with our house, we already have the picture of what it will look like when these sufferings finally end.

Actually, to be perfectly accurate, there is a big difference between those two things. With our house, we only have reasonable assurance that everything will be taken care of. Something more could happen to slow down the process. We live in Los Angeles. The big earthquake could hit and the whole neighborhood could be gone. We can't be 100 percent certain that our situation will all work out. We hope for the best. But such is not the case with God. He has promised that someday he will return and everything will be made new. God is infinitely more trustworthy than any insurance company. We not only hope for the best, we have been told and promised what it will look like.

> These are they who have come out of the great ordeal; they have washed their robes and made them white in the blood of the Lamb.
>   For this reason they are before the throne of God,
>   and worship him day and night within his temple,
>   and the one who is seated on the throne will shelter them.
>   They will hunger no more, and thirst no more;
>   the sun will not strike them,
>   nor any scorching heat;
>   for the Lamb at the center of the throne will be their shepherd,

and he will guide them to springs of the water of life,
and God will wipe away every tear from their eyes. (Rev 7:15-17)

The end is in sight. We have already been given a picture of what it will be like when Jesus brings an end to all suffering and pain. Then there will be no more hunger, no more thirst, pain, violence, injustice, sickness or death.

Ultimately, no matter what suffering we ever experience, someday it will come to an end. I love the promise that God himself will lead us to springs of the water of life and wipe away every tear from our eyes. We don't know the details of when or how. But we already know that one day all the suffering will end and it will be a beautiful day. No matter how bad things get, we already have a promise from a loving and powerful God. Knowing that helps us hang in there.

suffering
the pain just
sits there
nesting
till she finds a comfy spot
settling
the throbbing stills
and I walk on
knowing she's here
my companion

5

Freedom in Sexuality

KATHY KHANG

*I*t's a girl!"

I breathed a sigh of relief. Labor and delivery were finally over, and I was now the mother of a healthy, beautiful baby girl. I wept with joy as the nurses gently handed her over to me. "Does she have a name?"

"Bethany. She's Bethany. Welcome, Bethany. It's Mommy, and I love you," I said with tears streaming down my face. Bethany turned her head toward my voice and squirmed around in my arms until she and I found the perfect embrace as mother and daughter.

Hours later, all I could do was watch my husband rock and feed Bethany. Complications after childbirth led to emergency surgery. I was tethered to the bed by a series of intravenous lines. Drugs and hormones left me emotionally on the edge.

And when the relatives came, they pushed me over.

They commented on Bethany's full head of dark, thick, jet-black hair and her dainty fingers, then cut to the chase with two clear messages.

One: It was OK to have a firstborn daughter, because I was still young enough to keep trying for a son. Translation: Boys are better.

Two: My daughter was already a blessing by saving us money. She was valuable and beautiful because her newborn eyelids revealed deep creases—like mother, like daughter. We wouldn't have to pay for surgery. Translation: A girl can find value and worth in her appearance.

We Asian American women wrestle with issues of body image and our identity as women. Western cultural ideals of beauty are voluptuous blondes. We will never be that. But Western cultural ideals of Asian American beauty are often linked to Lucy Liu or Zhang Ziyi. We may look more like them, but they still represent unattainable, airbrushed ideals.

We cannot define ourselves solely on gender or ethnicity. We cannot be Asian American and ignore the fact that we are women. But as my relatives left the hospital that December evening, I wept. I needed to know and believe fully that God loved me as an Asian American *woman,* as his Asian American *daughter,* before I could look Bethany in her creased-eyelid eyes and tell her that God loved her for being herself—an Asian American girl.

I needed to know that God did not make a mistake in creating me as a woman. I needed to know God wasn't hoping for a son.

THE FALL

In Genesis, God creates and fills the earth and eventually commands Adam: "You may freely eat of every tree of the garden; but of the tree of the knowledge of good and evil you shall not eat, for in the day that you eat of it you shall die" (Gen 2:16-17).

The serpent twists God's words and asks Eve, "Did God say, 'You shall not eat from *any* tree in the garden?'" (Gen 3:1).

Eve's inability to remember the fullness of God's command leads her to add words God did not utter: "But God said, 'You shall not eat of the fruit of the tree *that is in the middle of the garden, nor shall you touch it,* or you shall die" (Gen 3:3).

The serpent homes in on Eve's uncertainty and presents the possibility that God is withholding something valuable and that what Eve has is not enough. "For God knows that when you eat of it your eyes will be opened, and you will be like God, knowing good and evil" (Gen 3:5).

Adam and Eve then open wide a door allowing Satan to twist all that is very good. Their actions exemplify what we as gendered, sexual people in this day and age constantly struggle with: the belief that God doesn't love us enough to give us the best, that he is withholding something from us, keeping something wonderful from us to hurt us.

As a result of the Fall, gender roles and traits became "assigned." Man is the strong one, entrapped in a moment of weakness, while the woman becomes the temptress. Humans' sense of intimacy with God and one another is shattered. Adam blames his wife. Eve blames the serpent. The relationship in which gender difference plays such a critical and essential role is broken because of sin. Instead of valuing and honoring one another, they turn against one another and against God.

How many times have I wondered if there was something else, something better for me than what God has given me? Many days I wish away what God has given me for something far less than a pearl of great price. I wish away my figure because I confuse being a woman with being buxom. I wish away my bridgeless nose because I confuse being a woman with being a Barbie doll. I wish away my sexuality—my inner sense of being a woman—for a fleeting and worthless sexiness that would flaunt my outward femaleness. I wish I hadn't been born a girl; I wish I could be the son my parents never had.

Adam and Eve, uncomfortable in their own skin, embarrassed of their bodies and at the sight of each other's, cover their nakedness with fig leaves. Their misunderstanding of God's gift of sexuality and gender is the first of many misconceptions future generations take to heartbreaking heights.

It's easy to blame Adam and Eve or even "the world" for our sexual brokenness. We can blame Hollywood for portraying the Asian American woman as impossibly demure and exotic or inherently able to keep her jet-black hair straight as she karate-chops the bad guys: we're either serving tea or kicking butt. We can blame the tabloids and television for today's image of women—highly sexualized yet almost childlike and naive. We can blame Madison Avenue and the advertising machine for image after image of women hawking underwear, dressed like angels strutting their wares down a catwalk.

Just the other week a catalog from a store aimed at girls in their "tweens"—ages eight to twelve—came addressed to my daughter. Young models wearing low-rise jeans and ultra-miniskirts graced the pages. Their glossed lips wearing slight pouts and their tilted hips saddened me. I wonder how much harder the Fall may impact this next generation. I confess: I threw out the catalog before my daughter ever caught a glimpse of it.

The hard truth is that we buy into Satan's lies. Just like Adam and Eve, we blame others. We are ashamed of who and what we are. We ignore the fact that we sin and that we sin against one another.

SHAMING AND CONDEMNING OUR SISTERS

Historically, Asian women have suffered simply because they were women. The cultural value for male babies in many Asian cultures is difficult to overcome. Agrarian cultures relied on the strength of males to tend the fields. Other cultures valued sons because the son was expected to provide for parents, while a daughter became part of her husband's family after marriage.

The objectification of women and our sexuality played out in World War II as women, and in many cases young girls, from China, Japan, Korea, Indonesia, the Philippines, Singapore, Thailand and Vietnam were kidnapped and sold into sexual slavery. "Comfort women" were forced into prostitution in military brothels in Japanese-occupied countries, in hopes that men with easy, convenient access to sexual satisfaction would be better soldiers and have less reason to leave the bases. The estimated numbers of comfort women range from twenty thousand to upwards of thirty thousand.

The legacy continues as prostitution and sexual slavery in Asian countries have branched off into their own tourism industries. No longer satisfied with shipping off their women as picture brides, Cambodia, the Philippines and Thailand have become the places to visit for those seeking sex with minors and teenage girls, according to a study conducted by Johns Hopkins University.

The presence of U.S. military bases helped build these industries in the Philippines, Thailand and South Korea. In 2002:

> Of the 41 major U.S. military camps in Korea, the 12 biggest are served
> by nearby "camptowns," where bar owners licensed by the Korean

government sell tax-free alcohol to G.I.s. (Korean civilians are not allowed in the bars.) Some 2 million customers visited the camptowns in 2000, the last year for which figures are available, according to Korea's Culture and Tourism Ministry. Troops at all the military installations in Korea are briefed on the consequences of engaging in illegal activities, including the one-year jail term that paying for sex can bring under U.S. military law.[1]

It has been estimated that 2 to 14 percent of the gross domestic product of Indonesia, Malaysia, the Philippines and Thailand is from sex tourism.[2] If visiting Asia for its rich history, architecture, art and scenic vistas isn't enough, you can tour an Asian country and visit local brothels. How Satan must delight in the fact that our Asian men and women are selling one another for something so common and worthless as money.

For those who find the idea of selling their daughters uncomfortable, medical technology has enabled people to avoid having daughters at all. The *Asian Pacific Post* reports, "A recent United Nations Population Fund report said the practice of gender selection is widespread in India, where affluent parents are killing tens of thousands of fetal girls per year, hoping for a boy instead." According to a 2001 census, the overall birthrate for India was 927 girls per 1,000 boys, a steady decline from 945 girls per 1,000 boys in 1991 and 962 in 1981. Based on those statistics, as a result of abortions or killing infant girls, up to five million baby girls "disappear" from India every year.[3]

China's one-child policy, enacted in 1980, was officially intended to curb the world's overpopulation, but it continues to have a profound impact on the country's women. I met a young Chinese American woman who was attending school in the Midwest. She talked about her boyfriend, their love for one another, their breakups and reunions, and their hopes for marriage. As I continued to listen, I learned that she had been left with relatives in China when her parents and older sibling left the country.

I fished for details to fill in the blanks, but even she was uncertain as to some of the facts. All she knew for sure was that she had been left behind because her parents could not immediately claim her as their child. There was a deep sense of shame, and she eventually articulated her feelings of being abandoned by her family.

"I hated America. I hated my parents. I hated school. I was 'extra' in this world . . . by law I'm not supposed to be here, an extra human being," she recalls.

It's a girl! But let's pretend she doesn't exist. Is that the message her parents meant to send?

This young woman and I tried to unpack the hurt that she had buried deep in her heart, the hurt that seemed to compel her to find intimacy, value and worth in her dating relationships. We prayed that afternoon for God to show her how much he loved her and would never abandon her.

It's a girl, and I will never abandon you! I hoped and prayed she would hear that message over and over in her life.

> *They probably do have an Asian Barbie.*
>
> IRIS CHANG

What kind of culture so despises its women that women would abandon or kill their own daughters? What might it look like if a generation of Asian American women believed they were beautiful, valuable and worthy, silencing Satan's lies and allowing God's truth to transform the world?

SINNING UNDER THE KNIFE

Before we can take action, though, we actually have to believe we are beautiful. I would have to believe *I* am beautiful.

Asian women all over the world continue to magnify Satan's whispers by willingly cutting and reconstructing their faces and bodies to achieve beauty. We are not content with what the Maker of the universe has given us, so we've planted ourselves at the feet of surgeons offering up our eyelids, noses, chins, cheeks, lips, breasts, thighs and even calves hoping that modern "medicine" can cure us of our bodies.

In China, Korea and Indonesia, where virginity is highly prized, women are racing to complete hymen reconstruction in time for their wedding night.[4] In Korea and Japan, women with *muu-dari* or *daikon-ashi*—"radish-shaped" calves—can have a nerve behind their knees severed in order to target a portion of calf muscle. With the nerve severed, a portion of that muscle will atrophy, thinning out the thickest part of the calf.

Here in the United States, it is still best to head to the coasts to have any plastic surgery. Asian eyelid surgery differs from your standard cosmetic blepharoplasty because it's more than pulling up sagging eyes. Asian eyelid surgery is meant to create my one saving grace—a creased eyelid. A surgery that once left eyelids almost comically creased has now become an art form, so that you would have to look at childhood photos to determine whether the creases are natural or surgical.

I would be lying if I said that I've never thought about plastic surgery. Granted, my eyelids are already culturally desirable, but I've wondered what a bridge on my nose would do for my glasses and my looks. And a few years back when my mother suggested I buy a padded bra, I just about made a beeline for the nearest plastic surgeon. The reason? I was already wearing a padded bra! My mother stood there in disbelief reaching for my breasts, violating my personal space, muttering in Korean, "How can a woman's breasts be so small?"

The memory still makes me laugh, but there are many days when I fall into the lies: *If only I looked more "American" I would be more valuable.*

Allen Counter, professor of neurophysiology and neurology at Harvard Medical School, researched mercury poisoning in children and found that in Mexico, as in other countries such as Saudi Arabia and Pakistan, most of the patients with clinical evidence of mercury poisoning were grown women:

> In every case, clinical questioning revealed that the women had used skin-whitening creams—many for years. In other words, these women had tried so desperately to whiten their skin color that they had poisoned their bodies by applying mercury-based "beauty

creams." Saudi, African, and Asian women were also using these skin-bleaching chemicals in a tragic attempt to change their appearance to that of *white* women.[5]

SILENCING THE LIES

God's design for us was to be male and female and to delight in who we are as gendered, sexual people. There is value and beauty in being a woman.

We were not created to be asexual and genderless. God's intention was to create human beings as male and female. We were to be sexual beings from the start. There in the perfection of the Garden of Eden, God "blessed them and God said to them, 'Be fruitful and multiply'" (Gen 1:28). God did not mean for us to bear fruit like a cherry tree. He's talking about sex and our sexuality as a gift; our gender is part of that gift.

God saw our sexuality, our gender, as a good thing he created and was pleased with. In the Genesis account we read about the completeness and goodness of God's creation. We are told in Genesis 1:4, 10, 12, 18, 21 and 25—six separate times—that light, the land and the seas, vegetation, the heavens, the creatures of the air and sea, and the creatures of the land were "good."

Then God created humans, male and female, in his image. He blessed them, told them to have lots of babies, not by budding or pollinating but through sex, gave them dominion over the creatures, and then "God saw everything he had made, and indeed, it was very good" (Gen 1:31). In calling creation very good, God is calling our sexuality, our maleness and femaleness, very good. Those inherent differences, physical, mental and emotional, all were and are very good only when manifested as male and female.

Why is it important for us to understand the Genesis account and its implications? Because we must know that it was God who created us as sexual beings. God gave us our sexuality, gave us the gift of our gender and of sex, and it was all very good. This is not something Satan came up with. It has simply become a way for Satan to grow our insecurities, our selfishness and our rebellious nature.

Even though modern American culture flashes sex and sexualized images at us without hesitation, culturally for Asian American Christians, the subject of sex and sexuality often seems to be taboo. "Christians, Sex and Intimacy" is consistently one of the best-attended seminars at an annual student training conference held by the Northern Illinois/Northwest Indiana division of InterVarsity. The weekend seminar was created, in part, in response to the sexual brokenness students were wrestling with. Year after year students have commented that this weekend conference was the first time they had heard Christian leaders place sexuality in a biblical frame-

I could barely talk about my sexual sin, but during one spring weekend in college I could no longer stay silent.

My then boyfriend and I had had a volatile relationship at best, but during the good times I felt cared for and important. He told me all of the things that I longed to hear but could never hope for or believe about myself. "Julie, you're beautiful." "Julie, I love you. You are amazing." The words coupled with the tender kisses ignited something in my body I had never known. I had only heard that having sex was bad. What I hadn't heard was that the kissing and holding would feel so good.

Every time we crossed another imaginary line of purity, I was racked by guilt and shame for making a bad choice and for being bad. Every time we would vow to "stay pure," and every time we would push the boundaries further, until one night I believed the lie Adam and Eve believed—God was withholding good things from me. A moment afterward, my desire to be loved by someone who saw me as beautiful was overcome by the same things Adam and Eve experienced after their sin. I wanted to hide. I was angry at my boyfriend. I was angry at myself. But though I knew the only way I could become pure again was to tell someone and to break it off with him, I didn't do either.

Finally, when our insecurities led to groundless accusations and then violence, I had to speak. I called a close friend, and she and her boyfriend drove me to and from the emergency room. Hours later, I returned to my dorm room with my right shoulder, elbow and wrist sprained, swollen and in a sling, and my girlfriends surrounded me as I asked them to come with me to the drugstore. I was afraid I was pregnant.

The test read negative, and I did what any normal person would do. I went back with my boyfriend. Why? Because I was afraid that no other man would want me given my history. I wanted desperately for things to work out so that, even though I wasn't a virgin, I was still with the guy I lost my virginity to. That is how deep the lies went into my heart.

Within the year, the pain of our cycle of arguments, breakups and reunions had tired us both out. What was left of me felt like a shell of a woman. As he walked away from me for the last time, I felt as if a light breeze could blow me away—there was that little of me left.

And that brought me back to a cycle I had lived out before losing my virginity—finding affirmation in the company of men. I didn't have to sleep with them. It was their attentive looks and kind gestures. It was my grasping at the hope that no one could tell that I was damaged goods.

I'm now years into a process of healing and accepting God's forgiveness. For me this meant telling my fiancé that he would not be marrying a virgin and seeing the pain in his eyes as he tried to process that knowledge. It meant dipping my toes in guilt and shame again when I couldn't get pregnant and thought God was punishing me for my sin.

It meant silencing the lies and clinging to God's truth: I am forgiven.

JULIE

work and then talk honestly and openly about sex.

For several years, I have felt like a fixture in the "Christians, Sex and Intimacy" seminar. The number of Asian American students registered for it is often proportionately higher than for other seminars; this has made it critical to include an Asian American voice among the teaching staff. Helping shape my talks were countless conversations with Asian American women about how they had had sex and felt "dirty" and undeserving of the love and respect of a Christian man. Others talked about their "secrets"—struggling with masturbation, wanting to have sex, having had an abortion, having been sexually abused by friends or family members.

One woman could barely speak a few words in between her sobs. Susan had attended church most of her life. She had given her boyfriend oral sex, and she was devastated. She recounted her sexual awakening—the first time they held hands, the first time they kissed, the first time she realized that she wanted to be physically intimate but was so afraid of "crossing the line." She couldn't even say the word *sex*. Instead of saying "oral sex" she pointed down to her genitals and then to her mouth. The most heartbreaking part of the conversation was at the very end, as her sobs slowed down and her face had an almost ashen look.

"I feel so alone."

As Asian American women, we grow up valuing community and a sense that somehow we are connected. When one of us fails, there is a deep sense of shame. We don't feel as if we just did something bad; we feel like *we are bad*. When Susan said she felt alone, she also said she felt cut off from her community. She wasn't sure if she could talk about sex within her Asian American community or her Christian community. She knew she couldn't talk about sex and sexual sin in her Asian American Christian community.

Why do we need to understand the Genesis account and all of its implications? Because if we don't there is no hope of forgiveness and of reentering community. Because if we don't go beyond the creation and the Fall, we are all alone.

REDEMPTION

Our bodies were not created with objectification in mind. Our bodies were not created simply for the act of sexual intercourse. Our bodies were given to us as gifts and healthy expressions of our sexuality and physicality. Taking care of ourselves, wearing that great outfit or fabulous jewelry, dancing and exercising, even our menstrual cycles all point to God's gift of gender. Ultimately, it's being comfortable with and even celebrating the fact that we are women.

Many times during my months of pregnancy I wished my husband, Peter, could be the one with the expanding uterus, sore breasts and fluctuating appetite. Empathy weight is one thing; looking like I had swallowed a watermelon whole was another.

The helpful, encouraging comments weren't helpful or encouraging. Even from the back you really could tell I was pregnant. I wasn't glowing. And that beautiful bundle of joy in my womb was just getting started in a career of sucking me dry of essential minerals and nutrients.

But I remember, a few weeks after giving birth, sitting in a brand-new glider rocker gently holding Bethany. I was falling asleep to the funny sounds she made as she nursed to her heart's content. It would be hours before I would step near a shower. I was probably wearing what I had worn to bed the night before, which was probably what I wore the day before.

It was the least sexy moment of my life.

And I thought how amazing my female body was, how creative God was. The breasts that Satan said were supposed to be bigger for me to be a real woman who could be appreciated by a real man were supplying everything my daughter needed to survive. As Bethany snuggled and sucked liquid gold from my breasts, I understood in a strange, new way what it means to be a woman in all of my body's complexity and beauty.

For a moment I understood that being a woman, a sexual being, didn't require me to be sexy. For a moment, I understood that God delighted in me, a woman, and I didn't want to be a man. I didn't resent my female-

ness. I didn't need to be a model. It was (and still is) incredible to be a
woman!

Not all of us have nursed a baby; some of us never will. That is not the
only way for us to embrace our femaleness. Otherwise giving birth or
nursing would be the only ways to get comfortable in our own skin. Finding our value and celebrating who we are as women requires God's help.
Remember, Adam and Eve tried to figure it out alone and covered themselves in fig leaves. It didn't work.

To cover their embarrassment, Adam and Eve needed more than leaves.
A blood sacrifice was needed to obtain skins to fully cover their nakedness.
Similarly, to cover our sin, Jesus shed his blood on the cross, paying for our
sin, releasing us from its power and restoring us to the Father.

Our sexuality, part of our identity as Asian American women, is a gift
from God, but we have twisted it into a broken shadow of what God meant
it to be. So we are called to flee from temptation and to walk in the path of
righteousness. Robbie Castleman writes that "human sexuality is redeem-
able. The denial of human sexuality is a rejection of the Redeemer's power
to overcome all the consequences and curses of the Fall."[6]

Being comfortable with and celebrating the fact that we are women requires covering ourselves—our hearts and minds—in God's truth. Psalm
139:13-16 isn't just words. Asian American sisters, this should be our song
of celebration. Guard your hearts with God's Word.

Being comfortable with and celebrating our womanhood also means we
need to understand how being a woman is different from being a man. We
need to understand our sexuality, to be comfortable with being a woman.

The closest my mother and I ever came to having "the talk" was days
after I had returned from my honeymoon. I wanted to tell her about the
exciting things Peter and I had done on our cruise, to vent early frustra-
tions after discovering the man of my dreams had flaws, to share the newly-
wed bliss.

But my mother wanted to have "the talk." Under the guise of asking for
help putting something away in her bedroom, she pulled me aside with one

purpose in mind. She was going to teach me about men and women, the birds and the bees.

"KyoungAh, men and women are different. Men need it more," she said. "That's just the way they are, and sometimes you just have to satisfy them."

My mother spoke in hushed tones in our mother tongue, guaranteeing that Peter would not understand a word if he by chance overheard our conversation. What I was supposed to gather from her obscure warning was that men and women are simply "different": men need more sex than women, and it was my job as the wife to satisfy that need for my husband.

That was it. My introduction to sexuality—days after I had returned from my honeymoon and years too late—took just a few sentences.

This year we will celebrate my daughter's eleventh birthday. She is becoming a young woman before my very eyes, and I reflect on how I always knew my parents loved me but were culturally unprepared to help me love myself as a girl and then as a woman.

I'm working on my version of "the talk." I want to tell Bethany that her body is an amazing thing that God put much thought into and delighted in. I want to tell her that God gave her body a rhythm and changes that can be scary but aren't intended to be. I want to tell her that her creased eyelids aren't the only or most beautiful part of her; it is the whole of her—her soul, her heart, her gifts and talents, her infectious laughter, along with her beautiful brown hair and big smile—that makes her beautiful.

God's design was to create us in his image, male and female. And he did this after creating a wonderful, strange world first. His expression of love and care for us came before the story of the great flood, the ark and the rainbow, and before any of humankind would know of Jesus. God's love for us started from the beginning in the creation of the world we live in. God's plan for our sexuality is partly to teach us deep spiritual truths about our relationship with him.

I want Bethany and all my Asian American sisters to know that God delights in us.

"It's a girl, and that is very good!"

naked
do you like my thick daikon legs?
juicy mangoes
on a tree trunk waist
would you like me better if I looked
like her?
will I satisfy
satiate?
and if I do
what does that make me?
a woman, desirable?
a *bad* girl?
I stand
staring at my boy hips
that don't hold the jeans just right
and tell the other women
airbrushed to perfection
to leave My mirror.
we stand alone
my reflection and I
satisfied.

6

Daughter of Two Worlds

CHRISTIE HELLER DE LEON

When I was sixteen, it dawned on me how similar I was to my father. One Sunday morning at a church service, I leaned back into my seat thinking about the speaker's message. My legs were crossed. My left arm rested across my waist, and my right hand was stroking the middle of my forehead. My posture looked like a distant cousin of Rodin's *Thinker*.

I casually looked to my left at my father, sitting down the row. Unexpectedly I noticed that he was my own reflection, but twenty-eight years older and masculine. Wide-eyed, I looked at him, then at myself, then at him again. His legs were crossed; his left arm rested across his stomach; he was stroking his forehead. I was shocked to see that I was a female carbon copy of my father!

No sixteen-year-old girl wants to discover the awful truth that she is exactly like her father—the person with whom she has battled many times about her physics grades, her responsibilities as an older sister, her curfew. Recovering from the shock, I quickly changed positions, hoping no one else had noticed.

A counselor friend once told me how important it is for children to individuate from their parents and forge their own identity. But I wonder if that is a Western way of looking at families. Western culture prizes being strongly individualistic. Time and again, I hear white American parents talk about pushing their children out of the house at age eighteen. This gives the children the chance to grow into their own identity, find their own way, forge their own path. I come from a culture in which family defines who I am. My parents taught me that honoring the family and duty to others—mainly family—is a way of life. Our deep loyalty to family is refreshing against the American backdrop of the rugged individualist. But there are times when loyalty turns to enmeshment. Getting so entangled in our families can keep us perpetual children.

There are both healthy and unhealthy expressions of individuation and family loyalty. Asian American women know this dilemma well. We want to be grown adults. We want to be good daughters. Our challenge as women of God is to find the healthy balance between the two.

UNDERSTANDING IS THE BEGINNING

Growing up, I heard many stories about my parents' childhoods in the Philippines. When my father thought I was watching too much television, he reminded me, "You know, in the Philippines, we had no TV. I had to climb up the lemon tree on the side of the house to watch the neighbor's TV." When we would visit Lola ("grandmother" in Tagalog), my mom told us that in Lola's younger years, she was the family disciplinarian-tyrant. "Your Lola would pinch me so hard on my side when I misbehaved in public. As she pinched and turned my skin, my face would twist. My eyes would always tear up," my mom said with a smile.

> *Before we can leave our parents, they stuff our heads like the suitcases which they jam-pack with homemade underwear.*
>
> MAXINE HONG KINGSTON

I confess it was hard to imagine my parents as children. But I laughed as they told stories that seemed so otherworldly to my Asian *American* ears.

Story after story revealed that they grew up in families that expected near-perfection from them. My father's stories were filled with phrases like "working hard" and "getting ahead." Accomplishment was in their blood. They learned from their parents and their parents' parents that doing well and being an excellent worker was the only way to be. Doing well brought honor to the rest of the family. In Asian cultures, where group identity is valued highly, accolades for one family member are accolades for the rest of the family.

I began to understand this concept at a very young age. In kindergarten my mother encouraged me to practice writing after school every day. She pulled the newsprint pages with the green dotted lines out of my backpack and coached me as I attempted to write my name over and over again within the lines, paying careful attention to the curves of the S's. My mother wanted to show my teacher, Ms. Laurel, that her daughter could print her letters very well. Good penmanship meant good parenting.

My parents' high expectations were rooted in Asian culture but were also part of their strategy for surviving in a new country. My parents had left the Philippines and joined the post-1965 wave of immigration, when the U.S. government eliminated immigration quotas and opened its borders to professionals, like doctors, nurses and engineers. With a suitcase, medical x-rays and their baby in hand, my parents left the islands for America in hopes of giving their children a life with more opportunities than they had had. They sacrificed much, leaving the safety of family and friends to begin a new life in a place they had only read about and seen on television.

As a child, I didn't realize my parents' first few years in the United States were so difficult. My mother and father tried to keep a good attitude and simply said to me, "Work hard." "Do your best." "Show 'them' that you can do it." As a child, I thought that "them" referred to my teachers or classmates. But now I know it referred to their new home, America. Show the Americans that you can do it. Susan Cho Van Riesen, a Korean American, writes about beginning to understand her parents' experience as Korean immigrants—what it was like for them to live through the Korean War and the rebuilding of the country's ruined economy. "As we gained perspective on their life journey, my sister and I began to understand why financial security was so important to our parents. They were not being randomly anxious about money. They simply had been deeply affected by their earlier experience of scarcity and difficulty."[1]

My parents and Susan's parents passed on to us their parents' expectations of them and their own immigrant hopes. Their drive to succeed would be our drive to succeed. Their resilience would be our resilience. Their shame would be our shame. As an only daughter for many years, I felt intense pressure to perform well in everything I did. My mother and father took turns teaching me what it meant to be a good and successful daughter in their eyes.

MY MOTHER THE TRUTH TELLER

"A mother's gaze is like a magnifying glass held between the sun's rays and kindling," says linguist Deborah Tannen. "It concentrates the rays of imperfection on the kindling of her daughter's yearning for approval."[2] The result is fire! And our Asian cultural values often add fuel to already complex mother-daughter relationships.

While Western culture encourages children to eventually relate to their parents as adult peers, Asian culture encourages children to stay children in the eyes of their parents. My non-Asian childhood friends grew up calling adults by their first names, setting the stage for eventual adulthood. But I learned that my parents were Mom and Papa and other adults around me, whether blood-related or not, were Auntie and Uncle. The titles indicated respect and also pointed to the fact that these people would always be my elders.

> *Whenever my mother talks to me, she begins the conversation as if we were already in the middle of an argument.*
>
> AMY TAN

Confucian thought, especially in the Japanese, Korean and Chinese cultures, reinforces the value of parental authority and honor. Children must always honor and obey their parents, no matter the age of the parents or the children.

When "true adulthood" happens for Asians is debatable. Some Asians believe that, for Asian American men, marriage rather than age is the marker of passage into adulthood—the point at which men begin to have responsibility to take care of their own families. Others believe that Asians, in general, are children until death. Tim, a Chinese American colleague, humorously commented once that not even marriage is the ticket to adulthood. "Your parents are still your elders and can treat you like a child," he said. "It's not even when they die, because then they are your ancestors. It's when *you* die. Then you can be the ancestor, too."

And the transition from child to adult is even more precarious for Asian American women. Our mothers want to prepare us to be wives and mothers. However, their attempts leave us feeling like children, even after marriage. I often feel like a child when I return to my parents' house. My mother comes from a long line of Filipina matriarchs who are not afraid to tell people what they think. My mother believes that it is her responsibility to teach me to be a better daughter, student, employee and wife. To that end, she has become my personal truth teller. Her method has been to tell me what she thinks at any time she believes appropriate and necessary: "Valerie got the award for best penmanship. Why don't you practice more?" In my twenties she would say in her lilting Tagalog accent, "Put on some makeup. You look so tired. How will you ever find a husband?" She compared me to herself. She would tell me, "Your cooking needs more flavor. It doesn't taste like mine." Though the words came from her lips like a song, they had a stinging effect. I found it very hard to please her.

Kathy, a Korean American woman from Chicago, recalls her experience of telling her mother her plans for a career in ministry.

> I was twenty-six years old, married and mother of one. I had spent four years working as a newspaper reporter. My degree was in journalism. I decided to work with a college ministry and floated the idea past my parents. My mom's response was "What a waste of your college degree! Why would you go work with college students with a degree in journalism from Northwestern? If you want a change, why don't you consider law school?" Often she would remind me that we don't have a "professional" in our immediate family—no medical doctors, no lawyers, no one "important" who could help our family. She would drop hints about hoping I would still consider law school or at least go back to school for a master's degree in something.[3]

Kathy's mother reminded her of the "truth" of the family: you are not important until you have a professional degree. Kathy was under pressure to bring not only money but also prestige to her family.

Another South Asian friend, Anna, spoke of her mother's desire for her to be healthy and in shape. Her mother's numerous "encouragements" ended up being comparisons to Anna's more slender friends.

All three mothers were well-intentioned in telling us what they thought. Mothers see their truth telling as a helpful gift to their daughters. Who else but a mother will be so honest with us? My mother attempts to love me by commenting on the gray hair that is beginning to show on my head, my fluctuations in weight and my cooking. She is my breathing mirror. She wants to improve the way I am because she loves me but also because my success or failure reflects on her own parenting. However, we daughters interpret their concerns as incessant criticism. Their words wound more than help.

GOING IN CIRCLES

I found myself in a cycle that was difficult to escape. I tried my best to meet my mother's expectations. There were times when I fulfilled them through earning high grades or simply doing things she asked of me. But there were times when I did not perform to her expectations. I didn't make the grade. Rather than going into a career in business, I chose ministry. Rather than dating a Filipino man, I dated a Chinese man. In those times, I felt as if her criticism of me grew louder. I would try even harder to please her, only to end up failing somewhere else. The cycle wore away my sense of worth. Questions filled my mind. *Am I worthy to be loved? Am I smart enough? Am I beautiful enough? Am I okay the way I am?* My mother's opinions affected how I saw myself. I wanted to feel that she loved me and was proud of me. Her approval meant the world to me.

The cycle of trying to fulfill my mother's expectations began to produce guilt and shame in me. My love for her and my desire for her approval pushed me to try to please her. When I could not meet her expectations, I felt guilty. I was not being a "good" daughter. I saw my goodness and worth as directly proportional to my ability to fulfill my mother's expectations. I was filled with shame as well. I did not want to be known as the bad cook or the poor student or the hardheaded daughter. I did not want to be an embarrassment to my mother or the rest of my family by being disobedient.

What I have realized is that it is unrealistic to base our value on attempts to please our mothers. The truth is that we will never fully appease them or meet all their expectations. It is impossible. If we try, we open ourselves to anger and resentment toward our mothers.

Scripture offers life-giving truths to counter the criticisms we internalize, and they help pull us out of our guilt and shame. Our mothers' expectations and words are intended to be helpful, but they need to be measured against God's kingdom values. It is not God's intent for Asian American women to believe that we are unloved, unwanted or undervalued. God wants us to see the value we have as his kingdom people, created by him. In Psalm 139, David expresses his awe at being created by a wonderful Maker:

> It was you who formed my inward parts;
> > you knit me together in my mother's womb.
> I praise you, for I am fearfully and wonderfully made.
> > Wonderful are your works;
> that I know very well.
> > My frame was not hidden from you,
> when I was being made in secret,
> > intricately woven in the depths of the earth.
> Your eyes beheld my unformed substance.
> In your book were written
> > all the days that were formed for me,
> > when none of them as yet existed. (vv. 13-16)

What I love about this psalm is that David knows who he is. He *is* God's creation. David reminds us that God is the master artisan who carefully creates everyone to be unique—our body types, the textures of our hair, the colors of our skin, the shapes of our eyes, our temperaments. Even before

God finishes creating us, he knows each day of our lives, what we will do and who we will become.

As we struggle to be good daughters and combat the negative messages about our worth, it is a comfort to know that every piece of the Lord's creation is wonderful. We are wonderful not because of what we do but because of who we are—daughters, lovingly created by God in his own image.

SEEING AND LISTENING DIFFERENTLY

Knowing how God created us helps us to view our relationship with our mothers differently. Whether they know it or not, our mothers are carrying their own mothers' expectations as they parent us. They carry the burden of being both a grown daughter to their parents and a mother to us. In our mothers we see ourselves and the mothers we will become.

I am learning to watch my mother. I am learning to operate, in Tannen's words, without my hyperactive "disapproval sensors" on. Not only do I want to hear her words, but I want to listen for the real message she is trying to convey. Rather than being suspicious of her words, I am learning the value of asking questions with humility and grace. "I'm not sure what's behind your question. Can you explain what you mean?" "Do you feel the same pressure I do, Mom?"

As much as my mother likes to talk about my weight, hair and complexion, she does give her share of compliments, too. I hold on to them gratefully. My job gives me opportunities to teach at various churches. I always look forward to teaching at my parents' church, because there, if I get nervous or lost in my notes, I can gather my composure and simply look out at my mother in the second row. Her encouraging face beams at me with attentiveness and pride. In that moment, even without words, I feel my mother's love for me. She is excited about who I am and who I am becoming.

MY FATHER, THE DREAMER AND THE VOICE

The media have more influence on me than I would like to give them credit for. The Disney Corporation had a tremendous role in teaching me about family relationships. Cinderella taught me that fathers and daughters are supposed to be close. Steve Martin in *Father of the Bride* showed me that a father dotes on his daughter and that his daughter will always be Daddy's little girl.

But as I grew up and worked with Asian American college students over the years, I noticed that the stories they told about women and their fathers were not as warm as the media portrayed. In real life, things like immigration, adolescence and generation gaps strain the father-daughter relationship.

In Carol's sophomore year of college, she was growing in her faith and wanted to take another step in growth. A Filipina American, she prayed and decided on going overseas for six weeks to learn about God's love for the poor. She was nervous about asking her father. He was hesitant about safety issues and about Carol being gone so long. In the end, he gave an adamant no. She yielded because she did not want to go without his blessing.

The following year Carol asked again. After months of her pleading and praying, and even a parent phone conversation with me, her dad reluctantly gave his consent. Throughout the process, it was clear that Carol's father had great difficulty in releasing control of his twenty-year-old daughter.

According to Christian psychologists Tim Clinton and Gary Sibcy, a father's role in the family includes being a harbor of safety, someone to be trusted, especially in times of trouble.[4] One part of this role is to create boundaries to protect the family. Clinton and Sibcy's view fits with Asian cultures well, as most are patriarchal; Asian fathers see setting boundaries and protecting the family as their important roles. Confucian thought elevates fathers as the key figure in the family. Asian fathers set the boundaries that should not be crossed or questioned. It is the family's duty to obey and respect the father without questions.

Conflict between immigrant fathers and daughters raised in America is inevitable. The father who used to benefit from being the unchallenged head of the household is now confronted with a culture that insists on free thinking and speaking up. Author and counselor Claire S. Chow says that Asian fathers may feel threatened when their daughters begin to think for themselves and make decisions that reflect their "freedom and self determination."[5] Disagreeing with one's father is seen as disrespect and an upset of the balance of power. A daughter's desire for autonomy can make a father feel useless or passed over. In my family, any attempts to question my father's reasoning or opinions were seen as mutiny. He had the last word on my education, my career aspirations, and who I would date and eventually marry.

My father kept a tight rein on our family, especially me. He was very protective of me because I was his firstborn and a *daughter*. My father's love was action-oriented. He showed his love for me by his investment in my education. In grade school it was not enough to get homework from my teachers; he would supplement that with his own homework—extra spelling words, geography, multiplication table recitations and algebra two years before the school's curriculum presented it. I was in disbelief when he tried to show me that there are letters in mathematics. It was unimaginable to the mind of a sixth-grader!

Unlike many Asian fathers, my father wasn't afraid to express how he felt. He was an avid learner and dreamer. He loved talking about what he was reading, what he was planning, what he wanted for his children. I realized later that my father's voice lingered in my head long after he stopped talking. It was difficult for me to distinguish his thoughts from my own. In high school I dreamed of being student council president. In college, I had dreams of being a businesswoman in a power suit, walking in tennis shoes to my power lunch meeting in San Francisco. Were these dreams my father's or my own? I noticed that white American fathers around me encouraged their children to dream. My Filipino father told me *what* to dream.

A FRESH START

I am thankful for my father's love and his desire to see me succeed. But there comes a time when the dreams and aspirations of a daughter diverge from her father's dreams and aspirations for her. Fathers may see it as a loss of their control and a daughter's rebellion. But for Asian women it means growing in freedom and finding a healthy independence. When we begin to venture out of the protective nest constructed by our fathers, we take our first few steps into discovering who we are.

My college years and my twenties have been years of attempting to understand my father and our relationship. Much of my growth as his daughter has involved learning how to manage some of my father's control over my life and to move in healthy ways beyond his boundaries. I had to keep reminding myself that my father and I were navigating through both an East-West culture clash and a generation gap. When I was a child, we wrestled and tickled each other. I asked questions; he answered. But as I grew, the words we exchanged became fewer and fewer. Communication with him was difficult. He spoke; I stayed silent, except for the occasional "Fine," "Good," or "Nothing." I knew that my father loved me, but in my teenage years I struggled to find my voice in my family, especially with a father who always had the last word. Even so, when he would make authoritative statements about anything and everything, I began to gather up the courage to respond by asking questions.

When I was seventeen, we finally had a confrontation that would change our relationship forever. That year I began dating my first serious boyfriend. My father was fearful of losing his daughter to a young man. He didn't want me to get hurt or, even worse, see me get pregnant. He began to tick off names of young Filipina women who had gotten pregnant and had children out of wedlock. "Do you remember what happened to Mary, Rachelle, Jennifer, Sheila?" he asked with disappointment in his voice. Though his list included just a few names, it seemed to go on and on.

I could understand his concern, since there was a high rate of teenage pregnancies in my hometown. But in comparing me to these women, some of whom were close friends of our family, my father conveyed a deep rejection of them and what I read as a growing mistrust of me. Despite all his investment in parenting me, he seemed to be saying, "Watch out, you will be next." With each name, my heart sank lower and lower.

I planted my feet firmly, even though my instinct was to run out of the room. A respectful daughter was not supposed to look her father in the eye. But after a long silence, with tears rolling down my cheeks, I looked up and yelled, "Why don't you trust me?"

I couldn't believe that I had just raised my voice at my father. But if I hadn't, nothing would have come out of my mouth. I would have stayed silent with my head bowed down.

Through tears and heavy breathing, I started reciting my list. "Papa," I said, "I am a good daughter. I've never done anything to break your trust. I am like a second parent to my brother, David. I serve Lola and Lolo (my grandparents). I've always done well in school. And I help out at church all the time. What more do I need to do?" With each item on my list, I attempted to remind him of who I was and win back his trust.

I had never spoken to my father this way. I think it scared us both. I didn't know what he would say or how he would react. I was preparing for the worst.

Then it happened. All defensiveness and anger suddenly dissipated from his face. Something clicked for him. With tears slowly running down his cheeks, he whispered the words I had been longing to hear: "You are right, Christie. I do trust you and I love you. Just please be careful."

We both stood for a while in disbelief at what had just happened. This was more than a taste of freedom; it was a deepening of our relationship.

I found my voice that day. It is angry and desperate at times, muffled by tears at other times, but it is my voice. I believe that that was the first time my father truly heard me. That conversation didn't make our relationship perfect, but it helped me to learn how to talk to my father as an adult.

A few years later, we had a difficult discussion about my desire to go into full-time ministry with college students. I was truly diverging from the path he had laid out for me. Our discussion was heated, but I had no doubt that he was listening to me intently.

Although he was opposed to my work in ministry, I began the fall following my graduation. My first few months on the job were difficult because I never received a blessing on my career choice. Receiving a blessing from my parents would mean that they were proud of me and that my work honored them. My father was appalled that even with a college diploma I had to fundraise a minister's salary. I attempted to honor my parents by allowing them to see my work with college students and faculty. I gave them chances to meet students I worked with. They heard me share about my ministry in front of church congregations. But despite my excitement about work with college students, they managed to bring up graduate school or a "real career" in almost every conversation.

About eight months later, I invited my parents to an event during which I taught a group of 150 college students. The invitation was part of my ongoing effort to help my parents understand my life as a campus minister. After I spoke, I ran to them to see how they were doing. My mother told me to check in with my father before the evening ended because she had seen his eyes begin to mist as I spoke.

I was shocked to hear that. I did not have the courage to ask him in person what had happened, but I called him the next day and asked what he thought of my teaching and why he began to tear.

After a short silence, he replied, "God spoke to me. As you were teaching, I looked around and saw how many people you are influencing. Then I heard God say, 'Let her go. She will be okay. I'm taking care of her.'" He went on to say, "I cried when God said that, but I knew he was right. So I said yes, I'll let you go."

My father let me go. At last I began to understand my parents' painful, yet necessary process of letting their children grow up. The night I taught, my father took another step of faith in his own journey as a believer. Like Abraham, God asked my father to trust him with his child's life. God asked my father to release control over me as a way to gain more control over my father's life. My father serves as an example of faith and obedience to me. I received his response to God as my blessing to stay in the ministry.

Unfortunately, not all fathers are willing to give up control of their daughters. I know of other Asian fathers who are emotionally distant. The fathers do not know how to express affection to their daughters. Other Asian friends were disowned by their fathers when they decided to enter professions that their parents did not agree with or marry people outside of their culture. It is very costly to stand up to our fathers. We risk being seen as disrespectful, or worse we risk being thrown out of our family. Yet when we don't feel heard or when we feel controlled by our fathers, we can easily fall into anger, frustration and even despair. This affects the ways we view God.

THE ATYPICAL FATHER

Many Asian American women, including me at times, have distanced and difficult relationships with God because of our relationship with our father. We see God as a controlling, stifling God who desires to limit our growth and freedom.

Thankfully, God cannot be contained in the father-boxes we put him in. Though our images of God are tainted by our experiences, I believe Jesus wants to show us a true picture of God as a tender Father who loves us enough to grant us freedom. In Luke 15, Jesus tells a story of a father with two sons. In defiance, the younger son asks for his share of the inheritance even before the death of his father. In Middle Eastern culture, the son's action is a horrid act of disrespect. Some biblical scholars say that the son's request implies a desire to see his father dead.

Whatever the son's motives are, whether selfishness or curiosity about experiencing freedom from his father, his disrespectful actions bring shame upon the father, the whole family and even the village. In a culture where group identity is strong, breaking relationship with his father means breaking relationship with the whole village. But with a grieving heart rather than anger, the father does the unexpected. He gives both sons, older and younger, their shares of the inheritance. He grants the request of the younger son and takes the risk of never seeing him again. Any other father in this culture would have disowned a son who showed such disrespect.

After the younger son squanders his inheritance on extravagant living, a famine strikes the land. The now destitute son hires himself out to local farmers of the land and works the most menial, shameful job there could be for a Jewish person: feeding pigs. Scripture says that in his despair, the younger son then comes to his senses and decides to return home. Expecting to be despised by the village for his offense against his father, he makes his long trek home. He remorsefully arrives home with nothing but a sincere apology and a desire to be a servant in his father's house.

"So he set off and went to his father. But while he was still far off, his father saw him and was filled with compassion; he ran and put his arms around him and kissed him" (Lk 15:20). The father turns decorum and social convention on their heads. He is unlike any father in the rest of the village. Compassion for his son makes the father break the rules of propriety to sprint toward his son. Out of breath, shamefully holding his robes up, with legs bared, he humiliates himself for his son's sake. No silent treatment. No "I told you so." No punishment. Instead, he welcomes his son back with a tight embrace and a kiss.

The son, who was ready to ask for forgiveness, never really gets a chance to speak. Before he knows it, the father begins preparations for a celebration in his honor. Kenneth Bailey, professor of New Testament studies, writes that Jesus "breaks all the bounds of patriarchal culture to present this matchless picture of a father who alone should shape our image of God as our heavenly father."[6] We serve a God who departs from cultural norms to love us lavishly!

The father in this story is the picture of God that we, as Asian American women, need to cherish. Many women have told me about being hurt by their father, whether by distanced and strained relationships or by abuse. The difficult relationship begins to inform their picture of God the Father. He becomes a harsh or untrustworthy figure, just like their earthly fathers. However, Luke 15 shows that God shatters the cultural boxes and inaccurate pictures we have of him. Unlike some Asian fathers, God encourages our freedom, even if it means not choosing for him. He does not turn a cold shoulder to us. He does not use silence to punish. God is a Father who loves with freedom, grace and reconciliation when we stray.

The father in the passage is a good model for our Asian fathers, too. I seek to encourage Asian fathers to see Confucianism and Asian patriarchy in light of our Christian faith. Both Confucianism and Christianity call us to honor our parents and to put the desires of others above our own. But Confucianism also clashes with Christianity. Confucius ideology relegates women to inferior positions. At every age they are to be obedient to men. However,

BEING ADOPTED

I am Korean, and I was adopted into a white family. What has been helpful for understanding my identity was hearing Ken Fong's talk from the Urbana 2000 missions convention about how we are adopted into God's family. It gave me a lot of comfort—a sense that an adopted family is natural and God-given. A lot of what I had heard seemed to convey the opposite.

I once heard that children who were given up for adoption will either place responsibility on their parents or themselves. I find this to be particularly true. I feel that even though I, mentally, know and say that I don't blame myself, the pain I feel comes from subconscious blame I place on myself. But in these thoughts I fail to see the reality that as a child I could not control the situation.

It helped me release some anger and feelings of abandonment, sadness and mourning for a family I'll never know. I struggled with some anger toward my biological parents and even my native culture because I felt abandoned. But I felt a need to suppress that anger lest I seemed ungrateful to my parents. I have found it helpful to talk to other adopted Koreans. I did an interview project for one of my classes, and I interviewed my cousin in New York who's also adopted. That was reassuring.

Being adopted has allowed me a certain freedom to redefine family in my own terms. I don't feel confined to let blood dictate who my family is. I have different close friends whom I see as family.

JODI KOHLMEYER

throughout the Gospels, Jesus shows his compassion for and empowerment of women. At times he elevates women over men as models of faith.

Paul Tokunaga writes about the necessity of choosing Jesus' teachings over Confucianism: "There are times when [Confucius] oversteps his boundaries as 'wise uncle' and we must point him to the door as an unwelcome guest. . . . As Christians, because we cannot serve two masters, we resist Lord Confucius and call only Jesus Lord."[7] There are times when, as in the prodigal son parable, deviating from cultural norms is a legitimate act of love. I long to hear more stories of fathers wrestling with their daughters' desire for independence and adulthood in light of Jesus' teaching.

While the younger son rebelled by approaching his father disrespectfully and selfishly, I believe we can approach our fathers in ways that do not dishonor or break relationship with them. Even though I chose a career path that initially seemed like disobedience to my parents, I tried to show them my desire to honor them. My parents knew that ministry is very time consuming and feared that they would see less of me. I made it a point to be with them as much as I could during my first year of college ministry. I stayed involved with my family while inviting them into my ministry tasks and decisions. These were small things that spoke honor powerfully to my parents.

MERGING THE WORLDS

Rather than write him off as an Old World authoritarian, I am learning to understand my father's perspective as a Filipino trying to raise his daughter in a culture that is not his own. Instead of seeing my mother as a hard-to-please matriarch, I am learning to understand her messages of love and concern. God upheld my parents through their journey away from their previous world in the Philippines, and he is giving them the tools to love and nurture my brother and me in this American context.

Like our parents, Asian American women have the task of living in two worlds: the world of dutiful daughter and that of grown adult. In the first world, we are daughters yearning to honor our parents well. In the second world, we are growing as leaders, making decisions in our workplaces, churches and communities. God shows us that living in both worlds is possible through him. He reminds us that we are *good* because we are God's creations, not because we have reached perfection. As we live in the tension of growing in freedom and honoring our parents, may we receive our Father's warm embrace and know he walks with us along this road between two worlds.

Parents
Embrace
push away
Enfolded
released
Tell me
no don't
Who you want me to be

7

Friends or Enemies?

ASIFA DEAN

You have 158 friends.

MYSPACE.COM

*A*sifa, you are so behind! How do you know what's going on? How can you keep up your friendships?" Some of my friends were recently teasing me because I don't have a personal profile on the Internet. After their initial shock about my being in the "dark ages" with modern technology, they schooled me on how to stay connected with my friends through the Web.

Having been thoroughly exhorted, I went home and thought about my friendships. *Do I have friends? Have I done a good job of keeping up with my friends? How do friendships fit into my life?*

I realized that friendships have played a significant role in shaping who I am as a person. Friendships have been hard work, painful at times, and have challenged my life assumptions. They have also been sources of great joy, companionship and comfort in hard times. Jesus has used friendships as tools to sharpen me as his disciple and transform my character. I consider friendships one of the greatest blessings that God has given me.

God wants all of us to have meaningful friendships. He commands us to be in relationship with each other. Jesus says, "This is my commandment, that you love one another as I have loved you. No one has greater love than this, to lay down one's life for one's friends" (Jn 15:12-13). Paul exhorts the church to "love one another with mutual affection; outdo one another in showing honor" (Rom 12:10). And in Ephesians 4:2 we are called to "lead a life worthy of the calling to which you have been called, with all humility and gentleness, with patience, bearing with one another in love." Relationships are key in God's design for us as people.

I will discuss some of the obstacles that we face as Asian American women in experiencing these deep God-centered friendships. This chapter will also highlight some of the blessings of being in a friendship with God.

FROM COMPARISON TO CELEBRATION

Many of my childhood hours were spent playing with Saima. She was one of the few Pakistani girls around my age in Redlands, California. We spent afternoons in the backyard making perfume out of smashed roses and pretending to drink tea from a fancy tea set. When Saima came over, I would eagerly perform a new roller-skating routine that I had created. I pretended that I was a figure skater, the cement in the backyard was ice and my one-piece leotard was really a beautiful ice skater's outfit.

I remember the summer that Saima got her driver's license. One hot afternoon, she picked me up in her new red convertible Bug. We drove to the mall with the radio blasting and the top down. Saima and I spent the day shopping, listening to music and talking girl talk. Saima was my best friend.

But there was an unspoken dynamic in our friendship—comparison. When Saima came over, I would compare what we were wearing that day, who was doing more extracurricular activities, who was getting better grades and who was more popular in school. Comparison was a thread woven not only through my friendship with Saima but through other friendships too.

I knew the criteria by which to compare: educational status, physical appearance, accomplishments, family background and relational status. I could tell you in a heartbeat what personal strengths added to my ranking on the invisible pecking order and which weaknesses dropped me down a few notches. I instinctively critiqued myself using these criteria and assigned myself what I considered the appropriate status in the ranking order.

A classic picture of comparison in friendship can be found in the book *The Joy Luck Club* between Jing-mei "June" Woo and Waverly Jong. Here June is recounting the history of her friendship with Waverly:

> Auntie Lin and my mother were both best friends and arch enemies who spent a lifetime comparing their children. I was one month older than Waverly Jong, Auntie Lin's prized daughter. From the time we were babies, our mothers compared the creases in our belly buttons, how shapely our earlobes were, how fast we healed when we scraped our knees, how thick and dark our hair, how many shoes we wore out in one year, and later, how smart Waverly was at playing chess, how many trophies she had won last month, how many cities she had visited.[1]

The friendship between Waverly and June is marked by both familiarity and comparison. They grew up together. They have been friends their whole lives. An outsider would probably guess that they are great friends. But in actuality June and Waverly's friendship is intertwined with an invisible generational battle of comparison. Their moms compared their daughters, and eventually the daughters began to compare themselves to each other. This was the same battle that Saima and I encountered in our friendship. And we both fell short in some area.

Comparison can take many forms. We may compare our weight, skin complexion, hair, clothes, families, whether or not we are dating, who we are dating, how successful we are in school, our spirituality, what kind of car we drive—the list is endless. A friend once told me that when she walks into a room, she immediately critiques what everyone is wearing and then ranks where she fits relative to the woman wearing the best outfit. Her ranking determines whether or not she's having a good day.

Comparison in friendship is a complicated struggle for most women; it may involve silently judging, gossiping, self-effacing and comparing our strengths with someone else's weaknesses. For Asian American women the struggle can seem to have more at stake because of the huge social implications. Exposed flaws can quickly lead to judgments of poor character, bad family and inferior ethnicity. It is a heavy weight to carry into a friendship. Comparison in friendships leads to envy, distrust, fronting false personnas and not being truly known.

Comparison also robs friendships of depth and celebration. I'm struck by Elizabeth and Mary's friendship in Luke's Gospel. Elizabeth and Zechariah, gray-haired, wrinkled and over sixty years of age, are expecting a child after years of longing for one. Mary, in her early teens, has just had an overpowering encounter with an angel of God, who tells her that she will give birth to the anticipated Messiah, Jesus, Son of the Most High God. After these remarkable encounters, Mary goes to visit Elizabeth.

As she greets Mary, Elizabeth is filled with the Holy Spirit, and the child in her womb leaps with joy. She recognizes the great blessing that Mary has received in being the mother of Jesus. Elizabeth happily declares that Mary is blessed among women. She considers it an honor to be in a friendship with Mary.

Can you imagine if Elizabeth had responded with comparison? Maybe she would have said something like "You're blessing is all right, but, to be honest, it's not as big a deal as my pregnancy at such an advanced age. By the way, what is your family going to say about your being pregnant?" Ouch! Or what if Elizabeth had been cold and remained silent to Mary's news? If Elizabeth had responded with comparison, the two women would have lost this divine moment of celebrating God's work in their lives.

Like a true friend, Elizabeth joyfully rejoiced with Mary and celebrated God's work in her life. Elizabeth had the great honor of confirming what God was doing in Mary and how he was using her in a special way. This moment gave all glory to God while also deepening their relationship.

God desires us to have friendships like Elizabeth and Mary's—friendships that celebrate each other, are hopeful about each other's life and confirm the ways God is at work in the other person. This is very different from ranking who is better or worse in a particular area. God-centered friendships focus on acknowledging and celebrating God's work in the other person's life.

My good friend Sabrina has been an Elizabeth in my life. Sabrina is opinionated and expressive; I am gentle and indirect. Sabrina is Latina; I am South Asian. We are different. I lived with Sabrina for three years while working as a campus minister at Oregon State University. During those three years, Sabrina celebrated God's work in my life. She regularly hugged me, kissed me on the cheek and told me how much she loved me. Sabrina jumped up and down with me in the driveway when I was given a car. Sabrina rejoiced with me when I got a promotion. Sabrina prayed for me and encouraged me with the truth of God's promises when I was having a bad day. My friendship with Sabrina was a form of sisterhood that helped me break free from comparison. It was a form of sisterhood that focused my attention on Jesus rather than on comparison and pretending to be perfect.

I'm learning that I'm able to let go of comparison by believing the truth that my value comes from God alone and not by how I compare with others. In *The Deeper Journey* M. Robert Mulholland Jr. says,

> There are two fundamental ways of being human in the world: trusting in our human resources and abilities or a radical trust in God. You cannot be grasped by or sustained in the deeper life in God—being like Jesus—until you are awakened at the deep levels of your being to this essential reality. You might describe these two ways of being in the world as the "false self" and the "true self."[2]

My true self is realized when I ask God to tell me who I am as his creation. And as I am in God's presence he tells me that I am loved as daughter of the Most High King. When this biblical truth becomes real to me, I'm able to celebrate who God has made me as his daughter. And because my identity rests in God, I'm free to celebrate God's work in others. This godly celebration both honors God and deepens my friendships.

THE BOTTOM WON'T DROP OUT

Another obstacle that friendships may face is a fear of being transparent. Asian American culture is a communal culture, so that both our successes and our failures are freighted with significant social implications. I know that when I meet someone for the first time, I am representing not only myself but also my parents, siblings and extended family. This affects my friendships. For example, growing up, I eagerly told others about the successes in my family—the awards my brothers received, the good grades, the huge family celebrations. But I kept the hardships hidden—pain within the family, financial problems and tensions between my parents and us kids. I would shame not only myself but the entire family if I told anyone about these struggles. I worked hard at presenting the "good" side of my life and hid my weaknesses and sins. Living under this fear kept my friendships from going deep.

Fear of being transparent with others leads to loneliness, deceit as we front a false persona, and shame. In Genesis 3, Adam and Eve wrestle with the fear of being transparent with God. They feel ashamed after they eat from the forbidden tree, and they fear to face God's response. Instead of being honest with God about what they have done, they hide from him.

The fear of being honest about who we really are leads us to hide both in our friendships and with God. We wonder if our friends would still love us if they knew the issues that we *really* deal with. *What will that say about me, or about my worth? Will I still be loved when my weakness and sin is exposed?*

God challenged me in this area through my friendship with Debbie. Debbie and I were college roommates; we led Bible studies in our dorm together and were excited to share the gospel with others. As we were walking through campus one night, I was eagerly talking about my week. Debbie was talking too, but I was talking the most. Midway in the conversation, Debbie stopped me and said, "Asifa, I don't feel like you are listening to me very well."

What? This was the first time someone had actually called me on my bad listening skills. "Yeah, it seems that when I try to say something, you turn the conversation back to you."

My face became hot. I could feel shame and embarrassment creeping to the surface. Debbie's confrontation exposed a flaw in my communication style. I knew that she was right. My listening skills were weak, and they didn't help our friendship.

I apologized. Debbie quickly forgave, and we continued to talk about all the great things that were happening in our dorm.

It was a defining moment for me. A weakness of mine was exposed, and yet the bottom didn't drop out. The world didn't come to an end. None of the things that I had feared would happen if my flaws were exposed happened. God was teaching me that night through Debbie.

Debbie and I were not building our friendship on hiding parts of ourselves. We were choosing to build our friendship on honesty and being known. In fact, after the initial sting of her exposing a personal flaw, my thankfulness for Debbie's gentle correction grew. I began to learn through our friendship that being honest with others and God about who you are is far better than hiding yourself in fear. Our friendship only got better.

More than this, Debbie's confrontation was not entangled with shame. It was different from what I had experienced growing up, where sin and shame went hand in hand.

Jesus had a perfect opportunity to shame a woman when her sin was exposed. Jesus was on his way to the Mount of Olives when a crowd gathered around him. Teachers of the law and Pharisees were publicly shaming a woman caught in adultery. They tested Jesus by demanding that he pronounce some sort of judgment on the woman. But Jesus didn't. Instead, he humbled the teachers of the law and Pharisees by pointing them to their own sin. Jesus then responded to the woman with truth and grace.

Throughout my thirteen years of actively following Jesus, he has prompted me to tell others about my weaknesses and sins. It's so countercultural! But telling my friends about my sins and weaknesses has been an act of obedience. Obeying Jesus has freed me from burdens of shame and

A LONG-TERM FRIENDSHIP

The year was 1979. The setup wasn't all that great for Geri Rodman and me to become friends, let alone lifelong friends. Geri burst into the campus ministry touted as an incredibly gifted leader from Canada. Even with three years of ministry experience and two years of overseas biblical training, I would be lying if I didn't say I felt intimidated and competitive.

But Geri and I were both eager to do the work among UC Berkeley students that we felt God was calling us to. I was on the front end of a new ministry focus—pioneering InterVarsity's ministry among Asian American students in northern California—and I needed and desired partnership help. Geri and I forged our friendship in the context of a staff/student household that grew as we ministered to students and developed new InterVarsity staff leaders. Now Geri and I have been friends and partners in ministry for more than twenty-five years.

My friendship with Geri has been an amazingly multifaceted gift from God. In this friendship, I have learned about being family and community in Jesus. Geri has a way of generously opening up her relational circles to include others. My household of long-term friends, non-Asians and Asian Americans living together, provided a rich transformative experience of community. To this day eight of us come together annually for an "Old Friends' Gathering," which has been a vital, yearly spiritual touchstone for me.

God used friendship with Geri and my other housemates to move me past some difficult relational patterns—for example, not easily identifying my feelings, let alone expressing them! Sometimes I expressed anger indirectly through passive-aggressive remarks or acts, because expressing anger toward parents and authority figures is simply out of bounds for Asians. I learned that it is redemptive to encounter "the truth in love," that on the other side I indeed encounter greater freedom and great healing.

My friendship with Geri has been a two-way street. I know that Geri is for me, and she knows that I am for her. Having survived my initial competitive feelings, our friendship has allowed us to be leaders that complement each other's strengths and giftedness. We have remarkably similar core values, but we are different people with some different interests. When Geri and I enter a bookstore, we head to different sections. Geri will go to the leadership and biography sections, while I'll head for literature and murder mystery. Our different backgrounds—American and Canadian, Chinese and English-Canadian—enable us to be multicultural in our outlook and in ministry. Geri and I are friends. We are a team.

DONNA DONG, DIRECTOR OF MULTIETHNIC MINISTRY,
INTERVARSITY CANADA

fear. I'm free to be who I am—a South Asian woman who is growing as a disciple of Jesus.

ARE YOU A SELLOUT?

Friends like Debbie and Sabrina have helped me mature as a Christian South Asian woman—even though they are crosscultural friendships. This can be a hot issue in our communities. *Is it OK to have friends outside of your race? Will you be seen as a sellout?* A South Asian friend wrestles with this tension on her college campus. If she spends time with non-South Asians, she feels judged as a sellout, untrue to her ethnic roots. At the same time, she doesn't feel as if her non-South Asian friends completely get her. She wonders if building friendships with other South Asians is just easier.

We can be pressured by our communities, our families and even ourselves to stick to our own ethnicity in friendships. It is easier to build a friendship with someone of your same ethnicity, and your ethnic identity won't get lost in the friendship.

But what we learn through Scripture is that God works through crosscultural friendships. We see this with Ruth and Naomi, Esther and King Xerxes, and Peter and Cornelius. God uses these relationships to heal, redeem and advance his kingdom plans.

I have spent several years involved with full-time campus ministry in the Pacific Northwest, but most of my South Asian community lives in California. Over the years I have often been asked, "Has it been hard to maintain your ethnic identity while living in a region where there isn't a huge South Asian community?" My answer has always been "Yes, but God has been healing my ethnic identity while being here. God has actually used my time away to help me understand who I am as a Christian South Asian woman." My friendships with non-South Asians have helped pinpoint some of the godly and ungodly aspects of my culture. I've been trying to model my life by the godly characteristics. My voice has also grown as a Pakistani woman through friendships with women who have Latina, black, white and other voices. And my love and understanding have expanded into wider dimensions of appreciation and compassion for God's world.

Brenda Wong, a full-time campus minister in Hawaii, says,

> As an Asian woman, I have gained tremendously in friendships with women of other ethnicities. In the last nine years I've had a deep and growing friendship with someone who is Hawaiian. Our worldviews and cultural values are often different and can cause clashes in our relationship. When I entered this friendship, I thought of myself as a flexible and loving person. But in contrast to "aloha," I had much to learn about loving others. I am learning to not just ignore the cashier or ticket taker; I can take the time to see them as people and fellow humans instead of rushing by them to accomplish my agenda.

Brenda's life is a great example of how God uses crosscultural friendships. Crosscultural friendships are actually a gift to us. They sharpen our own identity and help us to become more like Jesus.

Please don't get me wrong. I'm not saying that we shouldn't spend time with people from our own ethnic group. They can help us grow as disciples too. Friendships within our own ethnicity can be great gifts as well.

In May 2005, my dad went into the hospital with chest pains. He had already had a minor heart attack in 1997, and given his background of diabetes, I knew his symptoms were not good. After keeping him in the hospital for a few days, the doctors told us that Dad needed emergency open-heart surgery. Five of his major arteries were clogged.

My family was at the hospital by 7:00 a.m. the day of his surgery, even though visiting hours didn't begin until 9:00 a.m. Dad's surgery was scheduled at 11:00 a.m., and we wanted to make sure that we could see him before he went in. I was scared that day.

But God brought gifts for us. After sending Dad off to his surgery, my immediate family was told to wait in the lobby downstairs. There we were greeted by aunties and uncles, cousins, nieces, nephews and friends who came to wait with us. They took off work and school to wait with us for the entire day. They comforted us with their hugs and laughs, with chai thermoses and food, and with hope through prayer. It was just what we needed.

Looking around the room, I noticed my parents' close friends. They are uncles and aunties to me, but some of them had been grade school friends with my mom and dad in Pakistan! Their friendships have lasted through marriage, immigration to another country, raising bicultural kids and now illness. I was blown away by their friendship and loyalty. I thought, *These are the type of friendships that I hope for in my life.*

We can build friendships with people from all ethnic backgrounds. God uses our friends to bless our lives, bring us joy and help us become more like him.

FRIENDSHIP WITH GOD

The greatest friend we can have is God. The concept of God as a friend has often tripped me up, given my South Asian background in which respecting people in authority and elders is a huge value. I mean, my parents and elders are *to be respected.* I typically do whatever they tell me to do. If they want a cup of chai, I get it for them. If they ask me to run an errand, I rearrange my schedule to make it happen. If they give their opinion on something, it usually becomes the bottom line in a discussion. That's just how it works.

Growing up, I saw God this way: God created the mountains and the ocean. God has all power and authority; he reigns over the entire universe. God is the Almighty. God is the big G-O-D! He should be respected and obeyed. I saw God as a typical elder in my community, who shows love to me through providing for my physical needs, keeps me safe from harm and expects me to do certain things. But I didn't see God as a friend.

Scripture broadened my perception of God:

> For thus says the high and lofty one
> > who inhabits eternity, whose name is Holy:
> I dwell in the high and holy place,
> > and also with those who are contrite and humble in spirit,
> to revive the spirit of the humble,
> > and to revive the heart of the contrite. (Is 57:15)

God is indeed our highest authority. And what makes his authority particularly beautiful is that God, being who he is, desires to be friends with us. Scripture tells us that God lives in those who are humble in spirit. He is close. He is near. He is with us. God is a constant presence and constant friend.

God invited me to be his friend at a conference I was attending several years ago. God's Spirit was moving during an evening worship session. The leaders were inviting us to receive the gifts that the Holy Spirit had for us. Soon some people started to cry, others were standing still or bowing, and still others were receiving words of Scripture from God. I was like a fly on the wall—not so much out of fear, but not knowing where or if I belonged in God's presence. So I stood by the back wall watching others experience God's presence.

A few minutes later, one of the leaders said, "We believe that there is someone in the room who is deeply lonely and is not sure if they belong in God's presence. God wants to fill that emptiness." I immediately knew that I was that person, and so did some people standing next to me. Soon I was sitting and others were praying for me. In that vulnerable and powerful moment, God told me that he wanted to be my friend and take away the loneliness I had felt for so long.

Those words have stayed with me. Those words remind me that God doesn't want me to follow him based on duty and obligation. God wants obedience based on friendship.

I hope for all of us to see friendship with God and others as a part of God's amazing design for people. These relationships have the potential to be some of the greatest gifts in our lives. They offer joy and companionship as we follow Jesus. They are of great value, and we are called to steward them well.

꽃

Friends
My intimate
and chief rival
Living parallel
but otherworldly lives
When did we leave the same path
and become so similar?

8

Single Asian Female Seeking . . .

ASIFA DEAN

YASHOVARDHAN RAICHARD: *You didn't even once think about the background of the girl, her status, and her upbringing . . . how did you even dare to think that she could be a part of our family?*

RAHUL RAICHARD: *Where did I think, Papa? I didn't think at all. I just loved.*

FROM THE FILM *KABHI KHUSHI KABHI GHAM*

*K*abhi Khushi Kabhi Gham is one of Bollywood's bestselling movies. In this three-hour emotional roller coaster, Rahul, the eldest son of a prestigious family in India, falls in love with Anjali, a young woman from a poor family. Rahul is on cloud nine. His father is furious. Rahul's parents have arranged for him to marry a woman from a similar socioeconomic background. But instead of obeying his father, Rahul marries Anjali. The drama is intense! His new marriage is seen as such betrayal that his parents disown him and his new wife. The estranged newlyweds flee India and move to the United Kingdom, where they start a new life as immigrants. His parents' expectations for Rahul's marriage and future life partner are crushed. Watching this family cope with disappointment and shattered hopes is gut-wrenching.

Our Asian American communities have expectations about how we should date and marry. Perhaps it is being married by a certain age or to marry into a certain ethnicity or social class. Perhaps there is an expectation to put marriage before other priorities such as career or ministry calling. We live in a web of cultural assumptions about whom to date, when it is appropriate to get married, and what role we should play as a girlfriend or wife. But like Rahul, many of us do not fit perfectly into the cookie-cutter mold of cultural expectations. And that is just fine.

Whether we fit the mold or not, God is working in our lives on behalf of our best interest and his kingdom purposes. God is joyfully transforming us as disciples of Jesus whether we are single, dating crossculturally or married with kids. All of these life stages and situations are gifts from God and have equal value in his eyes.

This chapter includes stories of Asian American women who are at various points on the journey. They have experienced the unique joys and challenges of following Jesus while being single, dating crossculturally, being bicultural and being married. These stories are powerful testimonies of God's ability to work for our best interest as we follow him.

HAVE YOU MET SOMEONE YET?

Nikki Toyama

"Have you met someone yet?" One of the challenges of being an Asian American Christian woman is fighting the judgments that come along with being single: Is there something wrong with her? Is she too picky? Is she prioritizing her career over family?

It's difficult for me to balance being content with being single and being honest with God about loneliness. I feel I should be content with singleness—it's a gift that everyone has at some point. But at the same time, I wrestle with feelings of "less than" status in my church and among my married friends. Sometimes it seems my friends view my singleness as a problem to be solved. Sometimes I agree. But I don't think that's God's view of singleness.

I am grateful for models of healthy, strong single Asian American Christian women. They have inspired me to embrace my life. For a long time, I kept my life on hold, ready to be interrupted by the perfect relationship. But I felt convicted that I was putting marriage above following Jesus whole-heartedly. For a long time, I put stock in the assumption that the perfect romantic relationship would fix everything. But then a wise married friend told me that you bring your issues into your marriage—if you're lonely before you're married, you'll be lonely when you're married. Another person

SINGLENESS

All my life I have dreamed of being married and a mom. Today I am still single at fifty-one. Over the years, instead of just surviving the pain of seeing most of my women friends get what I want as I wait, I realize that God has also given me gifts in this lifelong struggle with singleness. My pain and disappointment have been gifts for me to find deep healing. I was trying to build my life and joy on something outside of myself. I believed that a husband and children would be my source of joy and satisfaction. With these desires unfulfilled, I gave myself to education, travel, friendships and helping others in need, but I was still faced with the pain of being alone.

My journey led me to find peace in being single because I am complete and whole in my relationship with God. I don't need anyone or anything to complete me. God has also given me power to take initiative instead of just waiting. I can enjoy the beach, a sunset, a movie, a party, good food, music and travel by myself, because I come to those things as a whole person with God and I am at peace with myself. I still hope to get married, but my picture of the significance of marriage has been transformed; I will enter marriage with more to give to my husband and family.

BRENDA WONG

gave me advice to use my singleness to "prepare" myself for being married—develop myself as a good person and become more Christlike. But after a while it felt as if I was putting my life on hold for something that I wasn't sure was going to happen.

I had just assumed God had marriage in my future, as a reward for faithful living. I have no idea where that idea came from. But seeing how God was using single Asian American Christian women helped me begin to understand that singleness is not a stop on the journey—it is also a gift. Ada Lum, for example, was one of the early Chinese American missionaries. She has traveled the world, starting Christian student movements in various countries in Asia. She still travels and teaches widely—she's known as a very powerful Scripture teacher.

In times of loneliness it is good to know God is there and will never leave or forsake me. I hold onto his words of love and tenderness in Isaiah 54:4-5:

> Do not fear, for you will not be ashamed;
> > do not be discouraged, for you will not suffer disgrace;
> for you will forget the shame of your youth,
> > and the disgrace of your widowhood you will remember no more.
> For your Maker is your husband,
> > the LORD of hosts is his name.

God's reminders help, because I forget often.

Single people have many gifts—time, energy, emotional availability and simplicity of life. We can contribute to the kingdom of God! I think these are God's gifts for me to steward. If I want to move to a different city, I just weigh the costs for me. But my married friends have to think about the effect on their spouse's job, the kids, the friends they have together, the community they are a part of. I have freedom of mobility. I feel challenged to steward this gift well—will I use it to entertain myself, or am I in a strategic place for God? Jesus' example—the way he shared his life with the disciples and ministered with a variety of men and women—shows me that a celibate person can have a full life.

BIBLICAL TRUTH ON SINGLENESS
Asifa Dean

Many of us are familiar with Paul's exhortation in 1 Corinthians 7:6-8 on singleness: "This I say by way of concession, not of command. I wish that all were as I myself am. But each has a particular gift from God, one having one kind and another a different kind. To the unmarried and the widows I say that it is well for them to remain unmarried as I am." Paul sees singleness as a good thing. Many of us have probably wondered why.

Our society would tell us that singleness is a good thing because we can do whatever we want with our lives. We can invest in ourselves. We can travel and discover the world. We can further our education or career. We can learn a trade or another language. It's all about us.

But Paul's reason is different. Paul valued singleness because it allowed his life to be at Jesus' full disposal. Paul's main priority was following Jesus. And since he didn't have the added responsibilities of marriage and family, he had total freedom to go where Jesus called him. Paul's reasoning for being single is more life-giving. It allows Jesus to fill our lives with purpose rather than us trying to fill our own lives.

I'm learning how to be a single woman who values singleness in the same way that Paul values it. When I hear Paul's words, I'm inspired and hopeful for my life. *How could God use me? What does God have in store for me? What are his great plans for my life?* I'm learning not to be apologetic but to ask Jesus what he has for me in this season. Giving Jesus my honest feelings and challenges about singleness also helps me keep a clear perspective, knowing that I am loved and that my life is meaningful. I'm able to hold on to the truth that being single with God is far better than trying to "fix" my singleness by settling for a bad relationship, filling my time with so many activities that I numb my heart, or walking around with an inferiority complex.

As Asian American women, we bring great gifts to God's kingdom. We are teachers, advocates, mentors, evangelists, leaders, pastors, prayer warriors, friends, activists and disciples of Jesus. God calls us to be a part of his kingdom! He isn't waiting for us to get married before we can be partners in his work. He doesn't see us as less because we are single. God's love for us is enough. His plans for our lives are good.

MEET THE PARENTS

Christie Heller de Leon

Growing up, I understood that my parents had a dating hierarchy for me. There was a priority order to follow if I ever had the opportunity to date. My parents would hint at an "OK to date" list. Of course, Filipinos were at the top of the list, while Caucasians and other Asian groups tied for the number-two position. Ethnicities that were not spoken about obviously landed at the bottom of the list. My Asian friends had similar hierarchies—their own ethnicity at the top, followed by other Asians and Caucasians, and Latinos and African Americans at the bottom.

Our families have reasons for wanting us to date within our culture. Keeping things "in the family" allows for fewer crosscultural misunderstandings. When we date people of our ethnicity and culture, we save ourselves from the pain of language barriers and cultural faux pas. Our partners are insiders in the culture and understand our traditions, customs and humor. My Asian friends say with a sigh, "It is just easier." On the other hand, our parents' or our community's desire for us to date someone within our culture may reveal ethnocentrism—the belief that one's own culture is superior to others. Prejudice or racism keeps our social networks closed off to people who are different from us.

When I was single, I was usually attracted to Asian men. Although I dated Filipino and Chinese men, there was still much learning involved. We learned about each other's customs, families and ways of communicating. I believe that these relationships prepared me for my husband, a white American of German and English descent, named Brian.

Brian and I met at a work training conference. I had never dated a white American before. As our friendship began to grow, I feared that I would be pegged as a sellout. I did not want to be another of the "Asian women with a white man" that I read about. Seeing Asian women with white men brought to mind mail-order brides and Asian self-hatred—women dating outside their ethnicity as a way to escape their own culture. I also feared losing my culture and language if I married outside of it. I wanted to be thoughtful about my dating decisions and not be completely swept away by my heart. Yet I found myself increasingly attracted to Brian. He was what I wanted: he is handsome, intelligent, respectful to my family, passionate for justice, and he has a wonderful laugh.

I solicited advice from peers and mentors about my crosscultural relationship. I prayed for God's wisdom to know if I should pursue it. I began

MEET THE PARENTS

Rhoda: At the very beginning, our parents were concerned for our relationship. They hoped that it would, at most, just be a nonserious dating relationship that would come and go. One reason was our different cultural backgrounds. Our parents did not think that two people from different cultures could survive in a marriage. They saw differences as a breaking point rather than an opportunity to grow. They also were worried about how our families would get along with each other. Both families have a tradition of gathering together for all kinds of occasions. Would my parents fit in at one of Eddy's parents' events? Would Eddy's parents feel comfortable if my parents invited them over? They knew that this marriage was not just about my marrying Eddy but two families marrying each other. My parents were also concerned for our future child. Since both Eddy and I are from minority cultures, they were concerned that our child would not get the same opportunities as a child who was at least half white.

Today we have started raising our kids in an American culture with an Armenian father and Japanese mother. This will be interesting! Of course we want our kids to know all three languages fluently, appreciate all three cultures and see themselves as 100 percent Armenian and 100 percent Japanese. The challenge will be how to do that well!

Eddy: During our engagement process, we were struck by the story of the Syrophoenician woman in Mark. The woman and Jesus have an interaction that on the surface level seems to show that Jesus is not concerned for her and for her family. But then Jesus honors her faith by his power to heal her daughter. Rhoda and I needed that word when we were experiencing a bleak engagement process. We needed to believe that Jesus would come through in a powerful way, when on the surface it did not look good.

One of the key positive factors was the way that Rhoda embraced my family and looked for ways to build trust with them beginning in the early stages of our relationship. She looked for ways to serve during family gatherings. Rhoda would also initiate conversation and contact with all of my family. It would have been understandable had her attitude been I'm not going to change for anyone, and if they can't accept me, then it's not worth it. But Rhoda practiced the principles and values of Philippians 2, choosing to love and to serve and build trust along the way. I love seeing the ways that my family has embraced Rhoda.

EDDY AND RHODA EKMEKJI

to ask God if this was the person he wanted me to date. I was hoping God would direct me very specifically. However, God rarely responds with the yes-or-no answers we often seek. Still, I gave him my concerns. *What would my parents say? Could we work through crosscultural differences?* As I laid my questions before him, he directed me to crosscultural married couples with grace-filled stories of learning and loving.

Out of many conversations with friends and family members, the best advice I heard from a mentor was that *all* relationships are essentially crosscultural. Each partner, even when the two are of the same ethnicity, has different family patterns. They have different ways of doing and ways of communicating to learn about and adjust to. There is blessing in crosscultural relationships. Different worldviews and perspectives enrich each partner.

However, with blessing there is challenge. Crosscultural relationships breed culture clashes. Brian tends to be direct in communication, while I am more indirect. Brian comes from a small family that values independence. When Brian left for college, his parents expected him to forge his own identity away from them. I spent my childhood with my immediate family and extended family. My college was only thirty minutes away from home. My parents expected me to come home every other weekend to be with the family. They believed that the family was integral in the formation of my identity. In Brian's and my dating relationship and eventually in marriage, our ongoing discussions have revolved around these differences—how to better communicate with each other and the role of family in our social life.

The most painful culture clash for many couples is parental disapproval. I have many Asian friends, male and female, who dated outside their ethnicity. They were truly in love with their significant other but desperately wanted to receive their parents' approval. As adults, they struggled to know how to honor their parents. Sadly, there is no formula for getting our parents to accept our partners. But what I admire about my Asian friends' struggle is their strong perseverance. They balanced deep love for their partners with a desire to teach their parents to open their hearts to new people. This is not an easy task.

Jeff, a Chinese American man, struggled through the years he dated Emily, a Caucasian woman, to win his parents' approval of the relationship. One reason his parents were adamant that Jeff marry a Chinese woman is that they had seen pain inflicted on the family when an aunt had married out. Jeff's father wanted to save the family from a similar situation. Jeff loved his parents and Emily very deeply. Five years of dating and not receiving his father's blessing felt like eternity to him. But those were learning years for the couple and Jeff's parents. Emily and Jeff agreed that Emily would learn Cantonese to communicate better with her future in-laws. Though their cultural differences brought family tension, both Jeff and Emily began to learn about and appreciate Chinese and white American cultures more.

Most important, the years of waiting led to more heartfelt conversations and letters between Jeff and his father. Jeff was learning how to be the adult son, rather than his father's little child. He learned how to not take his father's words as law but to listen, weigh responses and pray for God's wisdom. He began to see the sin of racism in the family. Jeff learned how to challenge his father in ways that expressed love and honor. At the same time, his father began to see his son as a grown man and thoughtfully weighed Jeff's words.

Finally, his father sat him down and said the words that Jeff had longed to hear for the past six years: "Son, God has changed my heart. Emily is a wonderful girl. I'm sorry for the things I've said or done to her. I hope to make it up to her in the future. Your mom and I are very excited about your marriage. We want to bless your wedding." Emily and Jeff were married six months later.

The picture of Jesus in Philippians 2 is my definitive example of a cross-cultural person:

> Let the same mind be in you that was in Christ Jesus,
>> who, though he was in the form of God,
>>> did not regard equality with God
>>> as something to be exploited,
>> but emptied himself,
>>> taking the form of a slave,
>>> being born in human likeness.
> And being found in human form,
>> he humbled himself
>> and became obedient to the point of death—
>> even death on a cross. (Phil 2:5-8)

Jesus left his heavenly culture, relinquishing his place at the right hand of God, to become human. He died on the cross for us. Paul calls us to be like Jesus in our relationships with others. He tells us to become servants, not looking to our own interests but to the interests of others. This passage reminds me that the risk of crossing cultures is leaving what is comfortable and known. But the gift is the opportunity to open ourselves up to new and different relationships that ultimately bless us.

Crosscultural relationships need to be entered into with the love that Christ offers us. There is much opportunity for mistakes and misunderstandings when we are in relationship with people who are different from us. We are confronted with differences every day. Clashes happen as we enter any relationship with people of other cultures. But we can rest assured that the love of Christ covers relationships with grace to continue to learn about each other, make mistakes, ask for forgiveness and keep growing together.

As a married couple now, Brian and I are grateful for the journey God is taking us on. We have received the blessing of friends and family on both sides. The risk of faith we took to be together has brought great blessing to our families and to us. Through asking questions, through laughter, through times of frustration and with a lot of prayer, we keep learning about ourselves and each other.

MORE THAN EAST OR WEST

Asifa Dean

My first year out of college, I wasn't ready for a committed relationship, but my parents were eagerly pushing me toward marriage. My parents had a long list of potential husbands around the world. Let's see, there was the Pakistani missionary in Africa. Intriguing, but bad timing. Then there was the computer guy in Philadelphia. Not interested. There was also an unknown potential in Pakistan. Not enough information. Getting married right after college seemed too quick a transition for me, and I fought hard for independence.

A couple years after college, I began to explore ways to honor my parents. Accepting their involvement in helping me find a spouse was an act of honoring. We agreed that they would introduce me to families who were looking for a spouse for their son but that ultimately I had the final say. So I entered into the awkwardness of arranged marriage with my parents.

Arranged marriages have been part of my family for generations. The concept is simple. The parents (or the eldest male) in the family look for someone who would be a good spouse for their child. Traditionally, if a suitable spouse is found and both families agree with the match, then the man and woman will marry, often without even seeing each other beforehand! The modern version of arranged marriage is more like the Western concept of a blind date. When the parents have found someone they think might be a good match, the two young people exchange pictures, letters, e-mails and perhaps phone calls in the hopes of getting to know the other person. If they hit it off, they proceed into a more serious relationship.

Several countries such as India, China, Japan, Iraq, Korea, Afghanistan and Pakistan practice the tradition of arranged marriage. Some Western countries are also now being exposed to arranged marriages due to immigration. My friends who come from a culture where arranged marriages are not the norm are both intrigued and shocked when they hear about my life. They can't imagine going through an arranged marriage process. As someone who has strong roots in two cultures—both Pakistan and the United States—I understand what they are saying.

In fact, one of the hardest tensions for me is the struggle of being bicultural. Western culture is captivated by the notion of romantic love. Millions of dollars are spent each year producing songs, movies and books selling the idea of romantic love. Don't get me wrong; I'm quite the sucker for a good romantic movie! Yet what I know about marriage tells me that a lot more than romantic love is required.

I am learning that God's way is more than just East or just West. God's way is found in the stories I read in the Bible—a way marked by total dependence on God and trust that God is working things out ultimately for my best and his kingdom purposes. God's way for me is found in the stories of Abraham and Sarah, Moses, Joshua, Elizabeth and Zechariah, and Ruth and Naomi.

Genesis 24 tells the story of Isaac and Rebekah. Isaac's dad, Abraham, orders a trusted servant to go back to Abraham's country to find a wife for Isaac. Abraham initiates, taking the father's role of helping his son find a wife. He does what he believes God wants him to do in the pursuit of a daughter-in-law. He sends his servant out to look for a suitable wife and trusts that God will give guidance. Both Abraham and his servant have to put their faith in God during this process. As the servant goes to the community well in Abraham's homeland, he seeks God's guidance. After he meets Rebekah, he continues to ask God for confirmation. And God answers the prayer of Abraham and his servant. This passage is profound for me because, ultimately, God is the matchmaker. He is the One who determines who will come into my life. My parents, my community and I are called to wait for God's guidance, trusting that he is working.

My parents see looking for a spouse for me as part of their job. They have explored South Asian connections to look for a spouse, as well as encouraging me to look for a spouse in my workplace. Although they would have preferred that I had married at an early age, I believe this process has challenged their faith to believe that God is bringing the right spouse for me and that it is worth waiting for God's best. My parents, like Abraham and his servant, are trusting that God is guiding them as they look for a spouse, whether he is provided through South Asian circles or by some other means.

STARTING A NEW FAMILY

Tracey Gee

When I was growing up, my mom was unusual in that she wouldn't let me do chores. I wanted chores, I asked for them, but I never got any. I'm not sure what possessed me to want chores so badly. Maybe it was watching reruns of TV sitcoms like *The Brady Bunch,* where chores were part of the routine of family life. Somehow I'd gotten it in my head that what I needed was a chore of my own.

When being choreless became too much for me to bear, I would go to my mom and beg, "Mom, could you please give me a chore?" Seeing that she was about to turn me down, I would suggest specific ideas. "Maybe I could be in charge of doing the laundry? Could I please wash the dishes?" I pleaded with her repeatedly.

But each time she would refuse and give me the same explanation. "Tracey, someday you'll be married and have a family of your own to take care of, and then you'll have to do the laundry and wash the dishes all the time. While you live with me, I want to do this for you."

From my mom's example and her words I learned a couple of things. I learned that it was assumed that I would get married someday. And I learned that when that day came, a lot of chores would be involved.

As I grew older, the assumption that I was supposed to get married became an expectation and a question. My mom began to not-so-subtly nudge me. "When I was your age, I was already married, you know. How much longer are you going to wait?" Before I even had graduated from college, I began to hear this refrain. I would try to explain to her that I was young, that people in my generation did things differently and that I still had plenty of time. But that usually didn't stop her from asking again a few weeks later.

When I turned twenty-five and wasn't married or dating, I began to put the pressure on myself. My biggest fear was that I would never get married because there was simply no one who had all of the qualities I wanted in a man. I wanted someone who was in love with Jesus, who shared biblical values with me. I wanted someone who would be 100 percent empowering of me as a woman and leader. In my mind, the problem with that was that I was attracted to Asian men. In moments of frustration and cynicism, I said, "An Asian man who is going to be 100 percent empowering of me as a woman in leadership? He doesn't exist!" I also wanted someone who could make me laugh. Oh, and it wouldn't hurt if he was a good dancer.

I was convinced that I would never find anyone to fit the bill. And God had taught me that it wasn't worth it to settle for just any guy. I remembered once hearing a speaker say, "Being single isn't the worst thing. Being in a bad marriage is." I took that to heart. Figuring that there just wasn't anyone "for me," I settled into hopeless resignation.

When I least expected it, one of my best friends, Benny, sat me down to tell me that he had had feelings for me for over a year. Unfortunately, out of pure shock, I laughed in his face and said, "But you're like my brother!" Then I realized how that must have sounded to him, and I quickly apologized. I told him I needed time to think about it. As I thought, talked to all my girlfriends and prayed about it, I realized that Benny was a lot of what I was looking for. He's even a good dancer! We started dating, and three years later we got married.

I had asked God for someone who would be 100-percent empowering of me as a woman leader, and Benny has been my biggest fan. He loves the fact that I lead, teach, preach and work with college students. He constantly tells me how much God loves me apart from what I do as a leader, but he also could not be more proud of me.

Like me, Benny is Chinese American, but his family speaks Cantonese and is from Hong Kong. My family speaks Mandarin and is from China and Taiwan. That in and of itself makes our relationship crosscultural at times. When it came time to prepare for being married, our cultures were telling us some things about what marriage means. Some of that was good, some of it wasn't. We needed to start learning how to discern the difference.

As our wedding date drew closer, I noticed that I was getting a lot of questions about my cooking. Did I cook? What did I like to cook? Did I know that you can cook this vegetable this way? Aunties were suddenly asking me all these questions. I had never seen so much curiosity about my skills in the kitchen. When I told them, yes, I enjoy cooking and want to learn more, I was rewarded with an approving nod and smile. "That's good," they would say.

I wasn't lying to appease them; I really do enjoy cooking. It's one of my favorite things to do. But these interactions were telling me that apparently being a good wife means cooking well for your husband. It also seems to mean doing those chores that I had dreamed about doing when I was a kid. On my wedding day, though, I joked that I had ultimately managed to fool my mother, because the man I had just married does laundry and washes dishes.

Cooking, doing dishes and cleaning for a husband—is there more to marriage than that?

The answer is yes. Chores aren't bad, but a strong marriage that is based on Jesus goes far beyond those domestic duties.

First and foremost, it's about servanthood. When Benny confided in our friend Jen that he liked me, she told him something that he has remembered ever since. Her advice didn't include dating tips about taking me to romantic restaurants or what flowers to bring. Her advice was "Learn how to serve Tracey. If you stay friends, you'll need to learn how to serve her, and if you start to date, you'll need to learn to serve her." Benny often remarks on how grateful he is for her words, because they have continued to shape how we think about our marriage.

Marriage is about servanthood. The aunties told me that it's about cooking and cleaning, and such chores are one part of servanthood. Am I going to wash the dirty dishes or leave them? Am I going to do the laundry with joy or with resentment? Am I going to help my spouse when he asks? Culturally, the trend is that the woman is the servant and the man is the one who gets to kick back and watch TV. In our house, we split the chores 50-50. That's not necessarily the only way to do things, but it works for us and who we are. It's certainly different from most models of marriage I saw growing up.

More than those specific acts, servanthood is a fundamental way of seeing ourselves: we are trying to serve the other person. I'm convinced that most of the time learning how to be a good roommate is better preparation for marriage than dating is. Being a responsible roommate, like marriage, is all about learning to serve someone else. Unfortunately, most of us have more energy for the thrill of dating than for the hard work of learning how to serve our roommates. But the latter is what great marriages are based on.

Second, marriage is about conflict. In general, good communication is important. Benny and I try to talk openly and honestly, and we talk about virtually everything. Some of that reflects our personalities. But no matter

BUILDING THE HOUSE

Growing up, I used to overhear
  Asian sisters.
They would say
you Korean guys—
all of you are tyrants.
One by one they dated white guys and I
  would watch the men,
defeated in a strange land with clay
  on their
hands and stoic eyes as if to say do you
  not see
the houses we were building for
  you with our own hands—
our parents carried the blueprints
  across an ocean,
did Solomon receive such a gift
  from David?
Our houses were small and slow in
  coming around
and there was rage in making them.

I guess I think about this right now
as I think about us.
To be reconciled
when everything about my sweat reeks
like a dash out of here, an elusive tactic.
I heard of a woman who said she knows
a piece of paper does not lend

father-healing—
it is not trivial right now that we should
timidly reach toward his cloak, even as
  the crowds
around us deem us aliens in their
  games,
hold us down and deliver us at the same
time in their mercenary ships—
we are sensed in the darkness and there
is power for us. Power in abundance
like myriads of butterflies that flutter
from the throats of gazelles in the forest
to swirl camouflaged with leaves.

How great love brings down kings
  and lords.

Linger with me, sister, a little
  while longer.
Suffer long with me, even as you
  deal with
the fact that it doesn't look like I
  know what
I'm doing—or, what does
  hammering over there
have anything to do with putting
  a roof over my head.

I want to press soft clay into your palms
   so that
you feel its coolness in your lifelines.
   My heart is a
sloe-eyed horse galloping. My hair—
dark mushroom after morning flood.

So I seek you out whispering
   community
in your ear when I have found you.
I imagine halls that contain our tribe,
a whole village to raise one child—
she who was sick and we stayed
   with her.

Still our hearts will be broken daily.
And we will be aware that weeping
is imminent on a night alone

in our beds. And yet we will open
doors to valleys we never knew existed
with our courage and witness a harvest
we could never have imagined. People
unspoken for will rise from the dead
and dance like indigenous chiefs
   in glory.
Because we were brave. Because we
   stayed.
And the rains—
the rain we waited so long for—
we will smell it in the air and grasp at
it with tears, as our torsos bend with
the weight of lush heart fruit.
Staked to our passionate Jesus,
his cloak around our shoulders,
his ring upon our fingers.

DAVE SIM

what, for a marriage to work well there has to be open and honest communication.

This becomes even more important in conflict. While we were dating, we dealt with a lot of conflict. In marriage, our conflict has become healthier, but that doesn't mean that we never fight. Conflict will always be there, but we can learn how to handle it well. As my friend says, we need to learn how to "fight fair," communicating with grace, openness and forgiveness.

I've heard a lot of Asian Americans say that they think of conflict only as a bad thing because of the negative ways that their parents or family handled it. Either problems were swept under the rug, or anger was expressed explosively. There was no model for dealing with conflict well. In their book *Fit to Be Tied,* Bill and Lynne Hybels say that in most cases spouses will "resort to the only conflict resolution procedures they are familiar with: the ones their parents used."[1]

But God can heal us from old patterns, and he can give us a healthier experience of conflict. We do not have to merely repeat what we have seen. Healthy conflict is one of the things that Benny and I have to constantly work at. The effort is more than worth it because it keeps disagreements, misunderstandings, sins and hurts from building up and lingering. Instead, we can fight but move on and even have a stronger relationship for it.

Third, when it comes to marriage, it's important to take Genesis 2:24 seriously: "A man leaves his father and his mother and clings to his wife, and they become one flesh." This understanding of marriage runs counter to the Asian way of thinking about marriage. Historically, women were the ones who left their families, and they were treated like second-class citizens in their husband's family. Often they were treated as little better than a servant. That was the right of the husband's family: she would be forever the outsider. That dynamic is still at play today in some parts of Asia.

Before Benny and I were married, we met with two friends whom we respected and who had been married for a number of years. We asked them to help us think about getting ready for marriage. With them we talked about topics like servanthood, communication and conflict. They brought up Genesis 2:24 and asked us if we were ready to leave our families and cling to each other. Other translations say "cleave," which means "to adhere strongly to." They asked us if we were ready to form our own family and give it primary importance over and above our families of origin.

Many Asian American couples never do this. They don't get enough distance from their parents, at the expense of their marriage. It is often especially hard for men to put their new family first, because culturally they are seen as an essential part of their family of origin. Many times they are expected to provide financially for their parents later in life.

Our friends emphasized that our primary loyalty needed to be each other. If one of us had a disagreement with the other's parents, we needed to defend each other and stick up for each other. We needed to put each other and our marriage first. Otherwise if we took sides with our own family of origin, it would divide us and slowly tear our marriage apart.

Heeding this caution doesn't mean that we don't care about our parents or that we isolate ourselves from them. Benny and I have had some great times thinking of ways to serve our parents together, and we really enjoy spending time with them. But it was important as we started our marriage to realize we were leaving our families of origin and becoming one with each other, starting a new family.

PUTTING GOD FIRST

Kathy Khang

One of the first parenting discussions my husband and I had after the birth of our first child focused on roles and expectations and how those would play out in the comfort of our own home versus the homes of our parents. Peter wanted the full experience of parenting short of what was physically impossible—giving birth and breastfeeding. He wanted to be a full partner, changing diapers, the eventual bottle feeding, bathing, cleaning up the spit-up.

But it had become clear to us through subtle and not-so-subtle ways— the disapproving glances, the comments about how unusual and odd it is to see a father changing a diaper and soothing a fussy baby, the teasing in Korean that they couldn't tell who the mother was—that culturally it was unsettling for older family members to see Peter do what I, as the mother, was expected to do.

I don't recall praying. I don't recall turning to Scripture for wisdom. We simply didn't include God in the equation and did what any modern-day Korean American couple would do. We avoided conflict with Peter's parents. We agreed that on trips home or when they visited we would assume the more traditional roles. He would enjoy a few hours of sitting around and being waited on while I helped cook and tended to our infant daughter.

And it drove me nuts.

But in some strange, somewhat sinful way, it was easier to avoid conflict, another cultural value, and eventually easier to continue following the pattern—honoring cultural expectations (because I already knew what those were) instead of seeking first to honor God in all that I am, do and say (because that would involve learning what I don't already know and maybe defy or redefine cultural expectations).

So the pattern easily went from putting culture first by trying to be the perfect Korean American wife to putting the needs and desires of others first: Peter, Bethany, Corban, Elias, and me if there was any time or energy left over. I incorrectly began to live as if the godly thing to do was to submit to the needs and desires of my husband and children first and die to myself. Isn't swallowing the suffering—putting personal dreams and goals on the shelf while I serve my family—what a good Asian American wife and mother does?

But the more I tried, the more it drove me into despair.

Make no mistake. I love my husband. He is my loudest cheerleader and fearless advocate. Over the years he has redefined the term *helpmate* for me—adjusting his work schedule so that I can travel for my job, pushing me to dream about what God might do in my life through leading worship, preaching, teaching or writing, encouraging me to be bold and dangerous for Jesus even when the culture says it's more appropriate to be quiet and invisible.

And I love my children. Bethany is the creative genius of the family, with a heart and soul of an artist; her smile and artistic endeavors take my breath away. Corban is the protector, with a heart so tender and curious; I delight in dreaming about what path God may have for him. Elias is the laughter in the family; he brings joy into whatever situation we may face.

But putting culture and family first meant God didn't always make a close second. The time I should have spent, could have spent and later wanted to spend, hearing from God was taken up living for my family and being as perfect a wife and mother as this Korean American woman could be.

And then it came: an invitation to participate in a leadership development program that would require time and travel away from family. It would require reflection on what God has done and is doing through me and in me, and what God may be calling me to be and become. I read the invitation through tears while sitting in the minivan with the two younger boys sleeping in their carseats while we waited for Bethany to finish school.

I remember a rush of questions in my head and heart. *Was God saying I wasn't a good enough wife and mother? Or that being a wife and mother wasn't good enough? Was God saying I wasn't a good enough leader? Or that I had to choose between being a good enough leader and being a good enough wife and mother?*

No. God was asking me if I trusted him enough to seek him and know him first, so that I could serve my family and maybe others from a well much deeper and richer than that I was currently drawing from.

Peter and I prayed, and we reached out to our community to pray with us and for us, before and after we made the decision that I would participate in the program. Others asked for help on our behalf, inviting help with the workload at home when I would be away. Peter, with the help of Latina, Andy, Ann, Stacey, Maureen, Greg and many others, changed diapers, washed sippy cups and chauffeured the kids to and from their schools and activities.

It was a new cultural paradigm that I fully expect God to continue shaping as Peter and I continue to walk in marriage and parenting our children through adolescence into adulthood.

"But strive first for the kingdom of God and his righteousness, and all these things will be given to you as well. So do not worry about tomorrow, for tomorrow will bring worries of its own. Today's trouble is enough for today" (Mt 6:33-34). In Matthew 6, we learn that God provides for his entire creation, from clothing the lilies in the field to supplying the needs of his people. This wonderful promise challenges us to put God first, even above cultural expectations in marriage and parenting. As we put God first, he becomes the main provider for our family's needs—including *our* needs! He serves us so that we experience his love and also can serve our family. What's great about God's resources is that there is enough for everyone, which means that we Asian American wives and mothers can also experience the life and joy that God offers.

JESUS AS OUR FOUNDATION
Asifa Dean

This chapter's stories show that, as we follow Jesus, he satisfies us and works good on our behalf within all life stages. We see that whether we are single or married, Jesus makes our life purposeful. We see that whether we are pursuing a relationship through Eastern or Western ways, Jesus' way is best. We see that whether we are dating someone of our own race or dating crossculturally, Jesus makes the relationship strong. He is the primary foundation of our lives and relationships.

The good news is that Jesus doesn't require us to date or marry within the set expectations of our culture. Instead, Jesus redeems our culture and offers the godly aspects back to us as gifts in our lives and relationships, while breaking us free from cultural lies and unbiblical expectations of romance. Jesus is the One who matures us so we can actually be in healthy and good relationships.

Jesus' perfect guidance offers many gifts for us as Asian American women, no matter what life stage we are in. We can trust Jesus to understand our honest emotions, to take care of us and to fill our lives with contentment. As Asian American women, we can hold on to the truth that Jesus' purposes for us are good.

༚

I am there
an ambiguous smile
a flirty touch.
I am there
long loneliness

and familiar solitary walks
with new wounds.
I am there
tender kisses on fingertips
his voice, *coming home soon?*
a hidden Post-it
stuck between to-do and numbers to call
You mean the world to me.
I am here.

9

Getting Used to the Sound of My Voice

NIKKI A. TOYAMA

When did you realize you are a voice?" The question caught me mid-chew. Around us the busy restaurant buzzed. Tortillas continued on their journey down El Macino. Forks and knives clicked on tile tabletops. Muffled conversations and an occasional laugh filled the room. But within me, something had stopped.

I leaned back in my chair and resumed chewing. The first chews kept the quesadilla from escaping. But when it came time to swallow, I didn't. *When did you realize you are a voice?*

The question came from Paula, the woman across the table. She was a strong leader whom I respected. I didn't know how to answer. Tilden and Mimi, two old friends, sat on my left. They stopped eating and waited. Chew. Chew. A sip of water.

Paula's résumé included an impressive list of experiences in the Christian and secular worlds. To me, she embodied Voice. Her anecdotes are filled with stories of "onlys" and "firsts"—the only woman in leadership, the first black board chairperson. To me, that was Voice—having presence, influence and authority. *When did you realize you are a voice?*

But who was I? If I made noises of agreement, it would sound like boasting. *The nail that sticks up gets hammered down.* So evasively I stammered some un-Voice-like response and quickly asked a different question. Even as the words came out, I felt my gut fold in on itself. I knew that I didn't believe what I was saying, but I said it anyway. Something like "Oh, I'm not a voice. And how is your family?"

Standing in the parking lot, we shivered as we said goodbye. "It was great to see you! Let's meet up again!" I hurried into the car, and rain started just as I opened the door. I glanced out the passenger window at the freeway, solid with red taillights. I shook off my wet jacket and settled in for a long ride home. The radio made noise, wanting attention. But I couldn't hear it over the questions in my head. *Am I a voice? When did I become a voice?*

SPEAKING IN PUBLIC

My parents always bragged that my first words came out in full sentences. As a child, I spoke like an adult. I skipped the cooing and baby-talk stage. Or at least that's how the legend goes.

Growing up in suburban Chicago, I continued to exercise my adult words. As an oldest child, I had plenty of chances to speak on behalf of my siblings—Katherine doesn't want her dessert, she wants me to have it. My family entertained constantly, and I often gave tours of the house complete with anecdotes. At church, I was the cute kid they asked to read Scripture for the Mother's Day service or to play a part in the Christmas pageant. In my family and church community, I felt comfortable speaking and had no problems being heard.

But even speaking had some rules. In my family, children were to be polite and not demand things for ourselves. We could be loud at play, but when it came to school we were to be obedient. If our opinions were different from those of the aunties and grandparents, we tried to figure out why we were wrong.

But school was a different story. My first bad grade (S- or "satisfactory minus") scared me. Long rows of S and S+ usually filled my report cards. But in the fall of third grade, I got bad marks for participation. A minus sign blotted my otherwise perfect report card. Earnest looks, good listening and following directions didn't count as participation. I had thought that I was participating in class—I paid attention, followed instructions and completed assignments. In my mind this was the behavior of a good student. But the teacher didn't think that my participation was enough.

Wanting to do well in school, I started to make myself raise my hand. I asked questions, whatever jumped into my head. I searched for an opportunity to say something, anything, in class. I spoke even if it meant repeating someone else or inserting a thought that didn't really connect with the topic at hand. It was hard. I had a tough time speaking without a good reason—I felt as if I was wasting class time. But my desire for a good grade trumped my internal angst. I figured out what others wanted and did it even when I felt uncomfortable.

That S- shook my little third-grade world. My journey outside of myself began. I now realized that my classmates and teachers didn't see me as my family saw me. At home, I was strong, daring and opinionated. At school, I was seen as quiet, diligent and obedient. I wanted to do well and quickly learned to play the game. So I ducked my head, worked hard and tried to stay out of trouble. I made myself speak once or twice in every class. Usually, I tried talking at the beginning to get "class participation" out of the way. In that season, I lost my voice.

Janet, a Thai woman from a mostly white community in Indiana, also lost her voice as a child. In her efforts to assimilate, she left her cultural identity behind and tried to emulate her white neighbors.

I knew nothing more than the Caucasian faces that surrounded me at school and in my neighborhood. I learned to reflect only what I saw in them and to become only what they exemplified to me. During my senior year of high school, a dear friend said to me, "Janet, I don't see you as Oriental. I see you just like me—white." I believe that was also how I saw myself.

Although my parents opened the first Thai restaurant in the state of Indiana, for most dinners at home we had lasagna, tuna casserole, or steak and potatoes. Not only did my peers see me as being just like them, but my mom and dad were also quietly forcing me to assimilate to the majority culture where I was growing up. Though Thai was their first and primary language, they would not speak it to me or teach it to me. They feared that I would not be able to learn English, and they were even more afraid that my English would be tainted by an accent and people would think I was stupid. I suppose I can't blame them, since they experienced racism in grocery stores, restaurants, car dealerships and everywhere else they tried to do business. My father was college-educated, yet people would look up strangely into his face as he passed, and then their eyes would follow him until they thought he was out of earshot. Insensitive drivel would then flow from their lips: "Why don't they go back to where they came from? Those people need to learn to speak English." With so much ignorance around them, it is no wonder they wanted me to blend in, to speak perfect English and to eat spaghetti instead of Pud Thai.

Asifa had a similar journey. In her Pakistani community, Asifa says, women communicate through laughter, serving and hospitality. The church meetings are large gatherings with food. The mother provides a spread of edible delights. She welcomes, feeds and makes others comfortable. After a time of eating, there's a prayer meeting. The men (or a head pastor) take the lead sharing and leading worship. He shares reflections on Scripture, but the women rarely lead. Instead, they serve chai and pass out dessert. Pakistani women are taught to communicate in a specific way. Their primary voice of influence comes through hospitality. Women are indirectly told that other kinds of communication are not needed.

In the process of discovering voice, Western values clash with Confucian values. Asian culture values discipline rather than rights, loyalty rather than entitlement.[1] In many ways, the Western view of voice is related to "standing up for your rights" and "asking for what you deserve." Both of these represent rights or entitlement. But the Confucian system holds loyalty to the group and discipline as higher values. It is not surprising that Asians have a harder time with the Western concept of voice. Add to that a communal mindset that doesn't encourage people to ask, "What do you want?"

But voice is not a Western concept only. What does it look like for Asians to have voice? Do they have to give up their values of loyalty and discipline in order to speak? Maybe loyalty is more altruistic than self-centered "rights" and "entitlement." Perhaps by looking at voice as *influence,* we may begin to discover what Asian voice, and specifically Asian women's voice, sounds like.

In my earnestness to be a good, diligent and obedient Christian, I listened to what others said a good Christian was. A good Christian shares her faith, so I tried to talk to my friends at school about God. I felt very uncomfortable sticking out, looking different and introducing such divisive topics. But I wore Romans 3:23 buttons on my backpack and tried to start spiritual conversations with my classmates. I was a reluctant but guilt-driven evangelist. I behaved as people told me I should. I felt like I was becoming less of myself and more of a Christian clone.

But it wasn't long before I found that God gave me a unique way of speaking, formed by my culture and my gender. I found this in Esther.

Queen Esther: For Such a Time

I learned about Esther at church when I was a kid. Queen Esther stared at me from my Sunday school's flannel board. Her cardboard cutout figure wore multicolored "Middle Eastern" clothing. Her sandals peeked out from under her royal garb. Her face, serene and slightly happy, showed the peace of those who follow God. She was a safe-looking woman, happy, who had faith in God. And her faith lead her to take a risk and speak up. God honored her request and saved the Jews.

But the actual story of Esther is grittier than that sanitized Sunday school version. Esther is an orphan who was raised by her cousin Mordecai. They had descended from immigrants who came to Persia against their will a few generations prior. When the king looks for a new queen, he conducts a state beauty contest—entrance into the pageant is mandatory. Esther wins the contest to be queen and is crowned. Under strict orders from Mordecai, she doesn't mention her ethnicity or her family back-

ground. Being an orphan and a Jew could cause trouble. Esther is silenced.
She has no voice.

She seems in a powerless position. Her ethnicity and family background
are liabilities. She is raped and then made queen. The king demands abso-
lute obedience or death. Esther has learned this lesson from his disposal of
the previous queen, Vashti.

Before, she did not have voice because she was a Jew and an orphan. Now
she is queen. In her official role, she still has no voice and no power.

Mordecai tells her of a plan to kill the Jews. He reminds her who she is
and calls her to action:

> Do not think that in the king's palace you will escape any more than
> all the other Jews. For if you keep silence at such a time as this, relief
> and deliverance will rise for the Jews from another quarter, but you
> and your father's family will perish. Who knows? Perhaps you have
> come to royal dignity for just such a time as this. (Esther 4:13-14)

Like a good Asian woman, Esther makes a plan that involves food. Her
petition begins with an invitation to dinner. During the banquet, she asks
the king to grant her life and to spare her people (Esther 6:3). At the risk of
her own life, she makes her request. The king intervenes in the genocidal
plot and saves the Jews. The very thing Esther had hid, her ethnicity, ends
up being a primary tool in the redemption of her people.

As a woman of limited means and resources, she did what she could. She
acted on behalf of her people. Her position gave her some access to the king.
She could invite him to dinner. She also had her ethnicity—and she spoke
up. God used her to stop a genocide.

The story continues. In Esther 9, Queen Esther coauthors an edict proclaiming a new cultural celebration for the Jews. She writes with full authority (Esther 9:29). Thus Esther goes from being a vulnerable minority woman
to an advocate and policymaker in the Persian empire.

Her story challenged me to think. If Esther, a rape victim, a member of
a despised minority, was able to speak, could I? Esther went from being

invisible (keeping her real identity a secret) to advocating for her people. Her inauspicious rise challenged me to think about the system that I worked within. I sometimes felt that my Asian American tendencies toward quietness and loyalty were more of a liability than an asset. *Have I been placed in particular places for such a time as this? Have my gender and ethnicity set me in the perfect place for—something?* I wanted to find my voice. I found it easier to speak when I knew that my voice was being used for others, not just myself. I started on a journey to find other women who used their voices.

OTHER WOMEN WITH VOICE

Jesus was resting in the home of a Pharisee (Mt 26:6-13; Mk 14:3-9). A woman comes into the house and enters the room where the men are eating. Weeping, she pours expensive oil over Jesus and washes his feet with her hair. She says nothing with her voice, but her actions cannot stop speaking.

Jesus comes to her defense when people criticize her: "Let her alone; why do you trouble her? She has performed a good service for me. . . . She has done what she could; she has anointed my body beforehand for its burial. Truly I tell you, wherever the good news is proclaimed in the whole world, what she has done will be told in remembrance of her" (Mk 14:6, 8-9).

The weeping woman's actions speak, and they continue to speak to this day. They remind the others that Jesus is going to die. She is honoring Jesus with her perfume. Her service and actions of discipleship are seen as acts of artistic beauty—Jesus says she's doing a "beautiful thing." She speaks loudly, without saying a word.

Phoebe, in Romans 16:1, is given the task of carrying Paul's letter to Rome. This later became the book of Romans in the New Testament. In this patriarchal society, it was very profound that Paul trusted his most theologically challenging letter to a woman courier. As the letter bearer, she does more than just carry it; she is also trusted to explain the letter. Just as a person might write down instructions and then orally explain them, Phoebe is entrusted with the ability to clarify if any confusion arises.

The more I looked in the Bible, the more I found women whom God had carefully placed. Esther used her influence to stop a genocide. The weeping woman used her presence and perfume to honor Jesus. Phoebe had authority as the letter bearer to Rome. Many women provided money or the homes in which Jesus conducted his ministry. These women represented godly voice: they used their presence, influence or authority to advance God's kingdom. They redefined voice for me: it is more than speaking out. They showed me that voice is not always noisy but it always has influence. Sometimes it is quiet and indirect—like me.

I found my voice, reflected to me, in the revolutionary literature of the Old and New Testaments. These women had voices, heard and unheard, that helped to shape Christianity.

God gave me a voice for a purpose. For a long time, I had used my voice but didn't feel comfortable with the sound of it. My experiences in school shattered my confidence. When I spoke out, my words seemed selfishly motivated. I despised myself for doing it. But through the women of the Bible, I began to reclaim the voice God has given me as an Asian American Christian woman. He gave me a voice for such a time as this.

REDISCOVERING MY OWN VOICE

During a visit to a medical device company in Japan, I discovered that my ethnicity and gender are gifts. I worked as an engineer overseeing projects for Asia. We toured a fascinating new manufacturing plant. It contained experimental technology, and my office colleagues were curious. They asked lots of questions: "What's this?" "How does that work?" After a while, our hosts started giving only vague answers. They didn't seem to like the questions the Americans were asking. Eventually, they didn't answer any of the questions that our vice president asked.

My boss was obviously frustrated, and he pulled me aside. He asked me to find out what I could. And I did. I walked alongside one of the host engineers and asked questions about the different devices. Our conversation flowed easily and casually, in contrast to my vice president's conversation. I learned about sterile manufacturing processes for medical devices and new plastics for use in hospitals.

By the end of the tour, my questions were answered generously by my host engineer. He spoke freely to me. I think he and the others had assumed that as a woman I wouldn't understand the technical aspects. (Ironically, I was the only technical person on our team.) In any case, our team was able to learn about different new technologies. My voice, as an Asian woman, was more effective than that of my white male supervisor.

In the work world, I was beginning to see some of the assets of my Asian female voice. But my inability to speak out as others did seemed an obstacle in my Christian life. Evangelism was so hard for me. I didn't identify with the people who stand on street corners and debate. I didn't feel comfortable bringing up religion with my non-Christian friends. I valued my relationships and connections with them too much to introduce such a divisive topic. In many ways, it felt as if qualities that were a part of my being an Asian woman were a liability for me.

Esther also thought that her being a Jew would be a liability. But it ended up being a gift. In the same way, I discovered that God has given Asian culture a voice that has its unique place and purpose in his kingdom.

On the Berkeley campus, I set aside a day each week to have spiritual conversations with non-Christians on campus. I always dreaded this day. One day I walked the two blocks from my home to campus. The clear, sunny skies did not threaten to cancel my plans as I had hoped. I started down the gentle slope of Bancroft Street. Terrified to go to Sproul Plaza, I made my steps as small as possible. I played games with the parking meters, weaving in and out as if on a cement slalom.

Sproul appeared a full five minutes sooner than I was ready. Around the plaza, crowds gathered for the lunch break. Students, staff and faculty sat on the steps, under the clock tower and near the student center. As expected, the area was full of antagonistic people who eat Christians for lunch.

"I don't want to do this." I confessed to my friend Grace. Bubbling with excitement, she was thrilled to spend lunchtime talking with people about God. I was not excited. *They will know what we're doing, and they'll get mad.*

Grace shook off my look of dread, said a quick prayer and then said she would meet me at the end of the hour on the other side. Emboldened by the fear of meeting Grace and having nothing to show for the intervening hour, I walked toward a cluster of youngish-looking students sitting on a green bench. That's when the roller coaster began. From people sitting on the steps in lower Sproul to others outside the administrative building, there was spiritual conversation after spiritual conversation. People were open and candid about their thoughts.

Afterward, I spoke with Grace about my initial fears—that people would be angry that we're talking about God, that we're Christians; that people would feel offended.

"Who would be scared or offended by *us*?" she said, gesturing at her five-foot-tall persona.

I looked down at my own five-foot frame. Part of what had opened the door to spiritual issues is that we don't look like stereotypical Christians to the campus. We could make challenging statements and people didn't feel threatened. We could talk about heaven and hell in a way that my five-foot-ten, Caucasian colleague could never do on our politically correct campus.

I laughed—Grace was right. My Asian culture had given me two gifts that could be used well for evangelism—a gracious way of bringing up hard topics and an unimposing reputation.

I found this same dynamic in a work environment. While working with a nonprofit organization in the Dominican Republic, I stepped into the middle of some tensions. The Dominicans had some questions about the integrity of the Americans running the organization. They noticed small acts of injustice and became very disgruntled. One day on site at one of the schools run by the nonprofit, Daniel pulled me aside and asked casually, "Why do all the Americans have a car, a computer and a digital camera? I should become a missionary so that I can also have a car, a computer and a digital camera." It was his way of pointing out that the Dominicans were not getting equal treatment. Being Asian *and* American opened up a unique place for this conversation to happen.

We function in a society that has clear perceptions about who Asian Pacific Islander women should be—quiet, demure, cute, not troublemakers. "I've decided to not call Asian women 'cute' anymore," my friend Celeste told me. It seemed an unnecessary courtesy, but as the months wore on, I noticed the wisdom of this. My small size puts me in a "cute" category, but it also creates barriers for people to take me seriously. It's frustrating how difficult it is to always confront someone's preconceptions. But I've found ways to turn such bias around. We can infiltrate places for the kingdom, and no one will suspect us. We are not seen as a legitimate threat, so people don't pay much attention. We can also say hard things to people—our small size or "cuteness" softens our message. This empowers Asian women to become great evangelists and prophets.

I used to think that the nonspoken voice of the Asian community served as a liability rather than an asset. But then I discovered the power of this communication style. I've noticed that when a group comes together to plan something, if a volunteer is asked for, not a lot of Asians will put themselves forward. But it doesn't mean that Asian American women don't take the initiative. Repeatedly I've seen Asian American women take a lot of initiative in practically invisible ways, whether it's going out to find more chairs for a classroom that's filling up or inviting someone who looks lonely to join the group for lunch. Asian women take the initiative to count all the people who are present and note who's missing. They notice when someone else is leaving. They take the initiative to write thank-you cards and pass them around in a group, or collect money for an appreciation gift. They take the initiative to bring snacks and create a hospitable environment. They take the initiative to be the scribe for group projects and do the typing.

I traveled to St. Louis to host a gathering for Asian American churches in the area. I had been advised to meet with a certain church's secretary, and it proved good counsel. She took the initiative to gather several women in the congregation, and for a couple of hours we talked about how to reach all the churches in the area. Women like these, who don't serve in "official" positions, have a lot of influence over what happens in the church. They have voice. The rest of the church would not know what happened in the board meeting over the weekend if one of these women didn't type the summary and put it in the weekly church bulletin.

Asian women's voices are key in the church, in companies and in the community. We need to recognize the ways Asian women already speak. But another important part is to notice and question the ways others devalue the contributions of Asian women. This may involve speaking in ways that are crosscultural in order to be heard.

I've come to appreciate the silent ways Asian American women voice their care and concern, especially in times of grief. Kathy also experienced this when her mother-in-law died recently and unexpectedly.

> I have some pretty vivid memories of learning how to be a good hostess—Mom teaching me how to peel and cut fruit, how to serve tea without being intrusive to the important conversations, the order in which I was to serve each of the guests, etc. My mom made it clear that it wasn't just serving food but that it was a show of how I was being raised, that somehow serving others properly would show the community that I was a proper lady. . . . She also explained that it would open doors of trust, respect and, of course, potential relationships. I always felt like it was a show . . . until my mother-in-law passed away. The Korean church tradition is that the day of death, church leaders, family and friends go over to the home of the deceased. It is the responsibility of the daughter or daughters-in-law to make sure these guests are fed and taken care of. I knew the rituals—placing a photograph on a small table with two white candles, tea, fruit, cakes, etc. I realized that I was serving more than tea. I was offering comfort and assurance to my mother-in-law's friends and family.

This became much more personal for me a couple of years ago. A good friend, Cynthia, died very unexpectedly. Her death caught us all completely off-guard. I had just received an e-mail from her a couple of days before; I was completely shocked. It was very hard to reconcile her death and her life. As a close friend, I found every detail of living during those days overwhelming. Small things, like getting dressed, maxed out my concentration. I don't remember anything from the days before her funeral.

The Asian women in my community kicked in, in force. Silent hands anticipated my needs and those of the hurting community around us. They saw, before we did, what we needed. The years of reading people and speaking nonverbally made them adept at ministering to our hurting circle. I felt paralyzed—I didn't even know how to pray. It was the Asian women in my circle who prayed for me and carried me till I could walk again. At that point, I looked at my culture with grateful eyes and saw the special gifts it brings to situations like this.

I've discovered that I have a voice. But I realize that others may not recognize it as voice. Sometimes I speak up and speak out loud. Usually, my voice comes in the form of asking questions that challenge others to think. I notice things—gender dynamics in a group, someone's dominance or a blind spot that needs to be addressed. One of my main avenues of influence is asking questions, in a group or on the side, that cause others to think about a significant issue. Other times, my voice comes through actions. This might mean advocating to give an "invisible" group of people airtime or creating projects that solicit voices of many people. When I use my voice, I think about how I can use it to empower the voiceless. That emboldens me to speak.

Jane Hyun helps Asian Americans navigate the corporate world. As an Asian person within a corporate environment, she emphasizes, we need to know our ethnic identity. There are many cultural values that we bring with us into the places we go, and it's important to understand what we bring in order to know how to communicate and function. "In workplace scenarios particularly, perception is often reality."[2] How others see you, whether or not it's accurate, affects how they will treat and evaluate your performance. Knowing that people will first perceive you based on cultural assumptions is helpful in managing your career.

Hyun continues, "An assessment of . . . how you perform is not based solely on the quality of your 'work deliverables' but also on how you interact with your colleagues."[3] Social interactions, how we treat people in authority, what is appropriate to bring up, how conflict is handled—all are influenced by our family dynamics as well as cultural dynamics. As Asian women, we need to understand our own identity and recognize the contributions that it makes. And even if others don't recognize the benefits of Asian values, it's really important to understand others' perceptions—correct or misguided—because in many contexts perception is reality. Managing others' misperceptions of Asian women is just as key as understanding our Asian culture in redemptive terms.

As Asian American women, do we speak up in ways that are natural for us? What is the Asian American female voice? The voice of some is loud and clear and heard above the din. We speak up, highlight issues and command attention. But we feel like outsiders, not being a "typical" Asian woman. Others have a quiet and subtle speaking voice. But will society recognize our indirect communication, our actions of service or our advocacy as voice? Or will we be dismissed as "nice, thoughtful Asian women"?

> *Normal Chinese women's voices are strong and bossy . . . everybody talking at once, big arm gestures, spit flying.*
> MAXINE HONG KINGSTON, THE WOMAN WARRIOR: MEMOIRS OF A GIRLHOOD AMONG GHOSTS

Speaking, whether loud and clear or through subtle, powerful means, is part and parcel of being an Asian American woman. It is part of our legacy. We continue a heritage of Asian American women who speak in a variety of ways. They may not feel "Asian," or perhaps the ways we speak are not heard as "voice," but they are a rich part of our legacy. Asian women have chosen to use their voices and their platforms to speak up—in words and actions—on behalf of others.

Janet's journey as a Thai woman has led her into service:

One evening there was going to be an activity in which we were going to divide up into our groups by our ethnic backgrounds. I was all of a sudden very uncomfortable. I had never been around this many

Yuri Kochiyama, a Japanese American, came to our campus for a celebration of Asian heritage. The smallest and most unassuming of the three speakers, she looked almost grubby next to the polished news reporter next to her. She gave her speech standing on tiptoe to see over the podium. I almost wanted to call it cute—except the power of her words silenced the auditorium. Her passion poured from her body, lifting her onto her toes. She pounded the podium but never yelled. She spoke of her experiences with Malcolm X during the Civil Rights movement. She was by his side when he was shot. Her advocacy work continues today as she champions freedom for political prisoners and reparations for black Americans. She leaned forward and called the audience to take action.

Kochiyama was born and raised in California. Her parents were Japanese immigrants, and she grew up in a sheltered middle-class family. During World War II, her family was relocated to an internment camp in Arkansas. After this experience she saw similarities between the Japanese American experience and the African American experience in the segregated South. "She realized that the senseless degradation and brutality that she and others experienced was the result of fear and ignorance caused by racism. Her commitment to eliminate racist assumptions and ideas became the focus of her life." Her journey from an apolitical citizen to a powerful social justice advocate had begun.

In 1960, the family moved to Harlem—a community thriving with political activity—and lived in a low-income housing project surrounded by Latino and Black families. It was in this new neighborhood that Yuri at the age of 40 began her political activism. . . .

Her political involvement transformed much of her thinking and actions. In 1963, she met Malcolm X. Their friendship and political alliance changed her life and outlook. She joined his group, the Organization for Afro-American Unity, to work for racial justice and human rights.

The murder of Malcolm X in 1965 intensified Yuri's commitment to work for dignity and equality for all people. Through her tireless efforts, she has challenged long-held assumptions about race and has advocated about the struggles of people of color in the U.S. and around the world.

THE LEARNING PLACE BIOGRAPHY CENTER,
www.nwhp.org/tlp/biographies/kochiyama/
kochiyama-bio.html

Asians in my life. I began to wonder what they would think of me and how I would act around them. But it turned out to be a sweet experience of peace and comfort that I had never felt before. They all spoke of parental approval, overachieving academic lives and people-pleasing issues. I left the room that evening thinking, *Those people really get me.* I was starting to uncover and appreciate deeper parts of myself.

Learning not to ignore the color of my skin, the heritage of my people, the uniqueness of the Thai people has brought a fullness of life that I didn't know existed. One is not better than the other; but both are gifts from my loving Father and Creator. As a Thai woman who grew up in the Midwest, I have the opportunity to embrace two very different cultures. I love cooking Thai food *and* macaroni and cheese. I still work in Indiana, but I spend summers taking students to Bangkok to serve the poor there and to experience a little bit of Thai culture. What joy and freedom comes from loving all of who God has created me to be.

As Janet has learned to appreciate her culture and find her own voice, she is also giving voice to the plight of the poor in Thailand by bringing others with her.

There are more than 100 million women missing in Asia, according to economist Amartya Sen's 1992 study. Comparing the relative survival rates of female children and male children in countries around the world, he identified countries with unusually low female-to-male ratios. Social factors in these countries apparently contribute to the mortality or disappearance of female babies. The countries with the lowest female-to-male ratios are all in Asia: Pakistan, China and India. Sen compared population numbers with the survival rate of female babies in similar countries. The most conservative numbers reveal 37 million in India, 44 million missing girls in China and more than 100 million missing in other Asian countries. Sen suggests that infanticide and neglect of health care and feeding are probably the main causes that so many baby girls die or are abandoned.[3] Since family restrictions (one-child policy) were enacted in China, many Chinese children have been assigned for international adoption. Almost all these babies are girls.[4]

Will anyone speak up for the missing women of Asia?

As a Japanese American, I realize my own contributions to the invisibility of other Asians. My friend Christie, a Filipina, has spoken about her own experiences choosing to be invisible in order to fit in. She felt invisible within East Asian circles. Asians often are lumped together, and the issues fought for usually represent an East Asian perspective.

Filipino students within the California university system wanted to make sure that the special needs of their community were being met. They also wanted out from the "Asian" nametag, so they fought to have their own separate box—"Filipino"—on application forms and student information records. Making this distinction created enough distance for this community to have its own voice and no longer be invisible on the campus.

Asian American women are part of a legacy of voice. Our history is filled with people who have influence and who speak up—in actions and words—to change society. These stories are often untold; noisy Asian American women are seen as not typical, while quiet Asian women are not seen as having a voice. Yet the voice of the Asian American Christian woman is varied and unique, powerful and influential. May we speak for those who are far more invisible. God gave us a voice as Asian American women for such a time as this.

Perceptions
small, cute,
quiet, harmless,

See Me

dangerous, bold,
beautiful, strong,
charged with
ancient wisdom
passed in the crackling static
of her thousand brush strokes
through my hair.

10

Becoming Leaders

TRACEY GEE

But I am not a leader!

A couple of years ago, I got an e-mail from a student named Erin at a small prestigious art school near the University of California at Los Angeles, which is where I work. She explained that she had attended the Urbana convention (InterVarsity's triennial twenty-thousand-person missions conference). Through that experience she gained a vision for her college. She wanted to see a multiethnic Christian fellowship established that would reach out to her classmates and fellow art students, even though the campus had a strong anti-Christian vibe. She was willing to meet me at a coffee shop near campus to talk about her vision and what to do next.

"I didn't think you were Asian too!" Erin said when we met. We got to know each other and talked about her experience at Urbana, her involvement at her church, her ideas for outreach on campus and with her friends. That year, we started a weekly God Investigation Group (GIG) on her campus. I told her I could lead the first few studies but eventually she would do it and I would mentor her. When it came time for her to teach, she protested, "But I am not a leader!"

Erin's view of herself and my view of her were so different. She had initiative, vision and big ideas. She regularly talked about her friends, how much she cared about them and how she hoped they would experience God's love. She had worked hard to get faculty sponsorship and support to make InterVarsity an official club. She boldly identified herself as a Christian when people tore down her flyers and made fun of Christians. She was willing to learn and was asking great questions. If Erin wasn't a leader, then nobody was.

I tried to be a mirror to reflect back what I saw in her, but her self-perception was cemented. She couldn't see what I could see. Instead she continued to insist, "But I'm not a leader!"

How many times do I think the same thing about myself? *I'm not a leader. Who do I think I am? I can't do this. Someone else should do it. I'll mess it up. I don't measure up. I don't know enough. I don't have enough. I am not enough.*

I go through this almost every time I take on a new leadership challenge. At first, when a new opportunity comes along, I get excited and say, "Yes, I'll do that!" I can see all the challenges. I can see the opportunity to risk, to grow, to see God come through and do something amazing, to make a difference.

Then as the program gets closer and the cold, hard reality of what I have agreed to do sinks in, I panic. I become exquisitely aware of everything I'm not. I want to quit. I want to run away. When it's particularly bad, I secretly pray, "God, I can't just back out now, since I did say that I would do this. So it would be really nice to get so sick that I have to stay in bed. It's the perfect excuse." I can't see the opportunities to risk, grow or see God do something amazing anymore. I only see the opportunity for everyone to watch me fall on my face, and I want to press the Escape button.

Self-doubt has become a normal part of my experience of leadership. And it is something that most of us Asian American women have to face. When I was chosen as captain of my dance team, I struggled with self-doubt. When I led a student prayer meeting in my dorm for the first time, I struggled with self-doubt. I remember sharing my fears with a white friend who said, "Really? It's that big of a deal for you?" Yes it was. When I gave a presentation to the board of trustees of my organization, I struggled with self-doubt. As I entered the room of Ph.D.s, presidents, pastors and executives, I nearly turned on my heel. When I took an intensive leadership course, I struggled with self-doubt and wondered if I deserved to be there or had anything to offer as a leader. When I gave a sermon for the first, second, third and tenth times, I struggled with self-doubt.

As Asian American women, we doubt ourselves. Overall, our brothers do not have to deal with self-doubt in the same way. Of course that is a generalization and there are exceptions. But when I asked an Asian American brother, Will, to step into a new leadership role, he hesitated because of time issues. When I told him, "Will, I see a leader in you," he sighed and said, "Yeah, I know." He didn't argue with me or protest as Erin had. He didn't doubt that he was a leader, he just didn't know if he wanted to give up other things to commit time to it. He didn't struggle with self-doubt as Erin did.

THE DOUBTING GAME

One explanation is that Will is arrogant and Erin is not. That is not a good explanation. Will is not an arrogant person. The difference between Erin and Will highlights the fact that women and men do not face the same things when they approach leadership. There are at least three reasons that women's battle with self-doubt is more pronounced.

Gender stereotypes. One reason is the messages we get about the meaning of gender roles. Psychologists have studied how children begin to receive messages about gender, literally from the day they are born. Little boys are called "strong" and "smart." Little girls are called "cute" and "good." Even before we can remember, we were probably receiving messages about what it means to be a girl.

Studies have shown that when little boys succeed academically, they are told that they are smart. When little girls succeed academically, they are told that they made a good effort. The opposite holds true as well. When little boys fail, they are told that they must not have studied enough. It's not about who they are. But when little girls fail, they are told that they must not be smart enough. It becomes something inherent in them.

Gender stereotypes are imposed generally but also culturally. Many of our Asian cultures do not affirm us as leaders. For example, Confucius stated that a woman's role is summarized in the Three Obediences: "When she is young, she obeys her father; when she is married, she obeys her husband; when she is widowed, she obeys her son." Men have authority over women until the day they die! Men have all of the authority, power and leadership. Women are merely to be submissive and passive. They do not carry authority, wisdom, vision or truth themselves. Paul Tokunaga describes the self-doubt that comes with being a woman as a "still small voice [that] keeps whispering, 'What you have to offer is not as good as what a brother can bring.'"[1]

Kepi'iluna is a Filipina Hawaiian who works for a private institution in Hawaii. She serves as one of four *kanaka maoli* (native Hawaiians) in a management position. In her role, she regularly corresponds with colleagues over e-mail. Once when she finally had the chance to meet some coworkers in person, they thought she was a tour guide who had come to show them around. They were shocked to find out that she was the supervisor. They assumed that an Asian American woman had to be a tour guide, not the person in charge.

Whether it's spoken or not, we get the message that it's all well and good for women to do certain things—be quiet and support other people's work behind the scenes. We do not get the message that we can be strong and capable leaders. We do not get the message that we should be listened to, that we can be supervisors, leaders or people of significant influence. Somewhere we have all heard it: "You're just a girl; you can't do that." When we face stereotypes that Asian American women cannot be leaders, another hurdle of self-doubt is raised.

Stereotyped in the church. Second, one of the biggest controversies in today's evangelical church concerns women in leadership. We face gender stereotypes in the world, and most times it's not any different in the church.

My friend Sadie talked about being in a Korean American church:

There's an unspoken rule that women are to be the quiet sidekicks of their husbands, even though they themselves have so much to offer.

Too many times I've seen the *sa mon nim* (pastor's wife) complex—a term I made up—with these amazing women put on the back burner to passively sit beside their husbands. In the Korean church, there's this stereotype that pastors' wives need to be quiet, gentle, submissive and able to play piano. A lot of times, although I may have suggestions or ideas, I don't voice them so well because of the fear that they will not be taken seriously or even listened to properly.

One Vietnamese American woman who had taken significant leadership with the youth group at her church said, "It's hard because the guys I work with say that they don't believe in women in leadership, but the reality is that I'm doing just as much if not more than they are. I'm not sure how to feel about that."

There is a significant theological debate in the church about the role of women. In many churches the two sides are sharply divided, the Bible passages on the issue seem confusing, and tensions run high. It is impossible to do those issues justice here since whole books have been written on the topic. However, my own reading and study have led me to the conclusion that God does call and bless women to lead. At some point each woman has to deal with this issue.

> While it is my theological conviction that women should be given the same opportunity for ministry as men, I affirm those who arrive at different conclusions *after* their study of Scripture has likewise led them there. It is critical—whatever position we take—that we not arrive at it via tradition ("it's what my church has always taught"), comfortability ("I'd rather not challenge the status quo and risk conflict") or sloppy exegesis ("these two verses seem pretty plain to me, so that settles it").[2]

Wherever you land on the theological issues, at the very least all women are called to be influencers to represent God in their homes, churches, families and communities. Not all women will become pastors, but we can all say that we are called to exercise leadership.

If by leader we mean one who holds a position of authority and responsibility, then every Christian is not a leader. Some are—some are not. But if by leader we mean a person who enters into a relationship with another person to influence their behavior, values or attitudes, then I would suggest that all Christians should be leaders. Or perhaps more accurately, all Christians should exercise leadership, attempting to make a difference in the lives of those around them.[3]

By that definition, a woman who is teaching a Bible study at church is exercising leadership just as a woman who is a manager overseeing employees at work is. A woman who advocates justice for others who don't have a voice of their own is exercising leadership just as a woman who is trying to influence her family and children toward God is. A woman who is trying to reach out to her neighbors is exercising leadership just as is a woman who is called to be a church pastor. A broad definition of leadership honors what God is doing through all the relationships, situations and arenas in which women are called to lead.

Because the biblical and cultural issues are complex, women who are trying to wrestle with them may struggle with significant self-doubt. It adds tension when we wonder whether God even wants us to lead.

Lack of role models. Also, we lack role models who are like us. One of the primary ways that people become empowered is to see role models of faith and leadership who inspire them. But we have very few Asian American women who are role models of leadership.

Every fall, I received new textbooks, new teachers, and promises to learn new facts and skills, but it was always the same story. There were no noteworthy Asians or women involved in the Battle of Bull Run, the Emancipation Proclamation, or the invention of the light bulb. While my lips were singing, "This land is your land, this land is my land" my heart was finding it increasingly difficult to resist the notion that this might not be my land after all. I perhaps was not meant to contribute anything remarkable to "my country 'tis of thee, sweet land of liberty."

Where were MY role models? With whom was I supposed to identify? Where were the prominent Asians in American history? Where were the women? Where were the Asian women? Why didn't my textbooks mention their triumphs?[4]

Subtly, we get the message that we don't or can't contribute anything. We can't lead. No one who is called a leader or who makes a significant contribution looks anything like us.

In the business world, the National Asian Pacific American Women's Forum reports that a recent research project documented the fact that the great majority of CEOs of Fortune 500 companies are male, heterosexual, light-skinned and six feet tall. I'm sure the same could be said of government leaders. In the church, there are several prominent Asian American pastors who are men, but we lack women of equal stature.

There are some exceptions to the rule. Andrea Jung of Avon, Jenny Ming of Old Navy and Indra Nooyi of PepsiCo are among the few Asian American women CEOs of Fortune 500 companies. Secretary of Labor Elaine Chao has a significant leadership role in the national government. Yuri Kochiyama is a Japanese American civil rights leader who worked alongside Malcolm X. We celebrate these talented women and the contributions they are making. However, the vast majority of the leaders whom we see and interact with every day are still people who do not look like us.

When leadership so often looks like someone else, how do I translate leadership values to who I am? I'm used to translating English words or phrases for my parents at times. I'm not used to translating this.

After I graduated from college, I went backpacking in Europe with a group of my girlfriends. We visited Westminster Abbey in London, the Louvre in Paris and the Sistine Chapel in Rome. We trekked from city to city and saw some of the most beautiful and most prominent examples of Western European culture. It was a great trip. I admired the landmarks, architecture and art.

Several years later I went to China with my parents. Visiting the Forbidden City, Tiananmen Square and the Great Wall felt markedly different from visiting Europe. In Europe, things were beautiful and inspiring. In China, things were beautiful and inspiring and *me*.

Both were great experiences. But there was a difference between seeing the culture that felt like me and the one that did not. Similarly, I see many examples of leadership that are inspiring. But as an Asian American woman I have precious few examples of leadership that are inspiring and *me*. When we don't have people like us to look to, it's harder to fight self-doubt.

One friend, Joan, noticed that she tended to discount herself at work even though she had seven more years of experience than some of her peers. She noticed that most of the Caucasian women in the office, even those with less experience and less knowledge, carried themselves with confidence, a sense that they knew what they were talking about. Joan pondered this: "I have given myself a stigma that is hard to get rid of. Why do I do that? Because I fear failure. I do not want to overrate myself, and I doubt my ability to pull off what my peers have."

At times doubt is much more than an internal reality. People don't respect us or question our leadership. That can be painful, and it can make it even harder to fight the self-doubt we already feel.

Terri, a Chinese American who works for Boeing, said, "My dad raised my sister and me not to use gender as an excuse for anything, which may explain why we're both engineers. However, it's hard to keep living that when it's very obvious that others around you don't feel that way about you."

When Jessica was a sophomore, she became chair of the On-Campus Housing Council, a group of about twenty-five student leaders from her university's residence halls.

There were times that year when one of the members of the council kept taking control of the meetings I was running, and kept second-guessing my decisions despite the fact that I was the only returning member on the council. At one point, I approached him about it, and he said because I led meetings more quietly and seemed to have so few opinions, he felt that someone else should step up. From my point of view, I was giving people space to talk, trying not to impose too many of my opinions and letting the group come to decisions together. That same year, our whole council had a major falling out, and I heard many rumors behind my back that if a more opinionated male had been leading the group, there wouldn't have been as much space for disagreement and things probably would have been handled better.

One of the most important lessons I've learned is that self-doubt does not cancel calling. That is, feeling doubts about my ability to lead isn't necessarily a sign that God isn't calling me to lead. Doubt and call are not mutually exclusive. In fact, in my experience they very much go hand in hand! But if we don't know that, we'll think we need to be completely self-assured and confident before we can move ahead. If we wait to be 100-percent doubt-free, we'll wait for a very long time. For many of us, self-doubt has been the default setting. It is something we need to face with God's perspective so as to not let self-doubt stop us in our leadership tracks.

JESUS EMPOWERS

Self-doubt can make it feel impossible for us to think of ourselves as leaders. It is frustrating, it does not seem fair, and sometimes it makes us to want to quit sometimes. But we are not left to overcome on our own: we have an advocate.

Jesus is our advocate. He advocated for women. In the words of Paul Tokunaga, "Jesus was amazing with women. They leaped over cultural and religious hurdles just to be around him. When he taught, he often used women as examples, never as the butt of jokes but as people with value and dignity."[5] He healed women, empowered them, taught them and befriended them. He wants to do that for us too. He is the One who gives us dignity and worth. He is the One who tells us not to be small in our own eyes. He is the One who heals and redeems us and invites us to become all of who we were created to be. Jesus is our best and most powerful advocate.

A great example of this is found in Matthew 28:1-10. We often hear this passage at Easter, but it has a lot to say to us as Asian American women in any season. Mary Magdalene and "the other Mary" go to visit Jesus' tomb, but there they get a big surprise when they face an earthquake, an empty tomb and a walking, talking angel. The scene is so overwhelming that the

It's unfortunately taken nearly two millennia for the body of Christ to recognize that Christ has shattered the shackles that have kept women and other disempowered people from being given authority to lead. Responsibility without authority is lame, and historically, women have been given all kinds of responsibility but hardly any real authority. I have seen firsthand how the Spirit of the Lord is raising up legions of passionate, bright and immensely gifted women. They need to see more examples of female Christian leaders.

For years, the body of Christ has asked the Lord to send more workers for the kingdom harvest. Isn't it standard operating procedure for the Lord to answer our prayers in ways that are completely unexpected and untraditional? I'm convinced that Jesus is answering our prayers for more leaders by giving us more female leaders, to rise up through the ranks to lead all manner of Christian and secular organizations. As a fairly established Asian American Christian male leader, I also believe that Jesus expects me to use whatever influence I have to open more channels of opportunity to these answers to our prayers. I for one am committed not only to giving female leaders chances to mature and contribute but also to enabling them with self-worth and self-confidence.

KENNETH UYEDA FONG,
SENIOR PASTOR OF EVERGREEN BAPTIST CHURCH,
AUTHOR OF *SECURE IN GOD'S EMBRACE*

guards "shook and became like dead men" (v. 4). The guards keel over, but the women keep going.

The angel addresses the women and first of all offers a word of comfort. He tells them, "Do not be afraid; I know that you are looking for Jesus who was crucified. He is not here; for he has been raised, as he said. Come, see the place where he lay" (vv. 5-6). He's giving them an orientation to the empty tomb. I can imagine that they are still in shock.

Then the angel gives them a leadership challenge of crazy proportions: "Go quickly and tell his disciples, 'He has been raised from the dead, and indeed he is going ahead of you to Galilee; there you will see him.' This is my message for you" (v. 7).

Now imagine that you are one of the Marys. You have come to pay your respects to Jesus. You are grieving his brutal death. The empty tomb is the last thing that you are expecting. And then the angel entrusts you with a message. It's not just any message—it is going to change the world forever. Jesus has been raised from the grave. You are supposed to tell the disciples this and give them instructions on what to do next.

The women have to leap some hurdles to do what the angel is asking them to do. At the time, a woman's testimony wasn't considered good enough to mean anything in a court of law. In that society and culture, being a woman meant being much less than a man. But God sent this angel to entrust these women with a crucial, unbelievable message! Whether or not they see themselves as the right messengers, they are now the ones God has chosen.

Many times God sends us an "angel"—a messenger to call us to step up in ways that we would have never imagined for ourselves. Such messengers can see beyond what we can see. They can see what God is doing in a way that we cannot, and they call us into boldness. God has had to send me many angels to get through to me and call me to tasks that I thought were beyond me.

It was my third week of full-time college ministry. The school year had just barely started. I barely felt like I knew what I was doing, but I was diving into ministry and taking new risks. Then my team leader, Doug, a Caucasian man, took me to McDonald's for lunch. I thought that it was just a regular supervision session and that we would talk about how my ministry had been going that week.

But as we were eating our French fries, Doug suddenly started quoting the movie *Men in Black* to me. He said, "I haven't been raising up a partner. I've been raising up a replacement."

Confused, I looked at him for a moment, trying to figure out what on earth he meant by that remark. *Why is Doug quoting a Will Smith movie?* He then told me that he had decided to move on from being the team leader, and he invited me to be his replacement.

Under Doug's leadership, the ministry at UCLA had grown from a small group of people to a fellowship of nearly 150. He had pioneered many new tools for evangelism and racial reconciliation. I looked up to him, and now I was being asked to fill his shoes. Twenty-five at the time, I considered myself much too young for such a responsibility. I would have never thought that I could become UCLA's team leader until God sent Doug to call me to step up.

All of my self-doubt, fears and insecurities instantly surfaced, but I saw that Doug believed in me and thought that God could use me in that way. Sometimes God sends us "angels" to call us to things that we thought were beyond us. Maybe you have had an angel or two in your life. I wouldn't be a leader in the way that I am now without people like Doug who called me to step up.

Here we also see that being a *messenger* is at the heart what it means to be a leader. We are not the message. *We are merely the messengers.* I think that sometimes the reason we get so scared is that we confuse the two. We think we are the message, and we see our weaknesses and inadequacies. But the real message is Jesus and what he is saying. He entrusts that to us even in our weaknesses and inadequacies.

After Jesus' resurrection, it is women who are chosen as the first messengers. They would not have considered themselves ideal messengers, but God chooses them. You may think that God would be better off choosing someone else, but I guarantee that God will call *you* and entrust you with a message. He entrusted to the two Marys the world-changing message that Jesus was alive. What message is he entrusting to you? How is he sending you out as an ambassador of the kingdom?

FEAR AND JOY

"So they left the tomb quickly with fear and great joy, and ran to tell his disciples" (Mt 28:8). I am so glad Matthew tells us what the women are feeling. The words are *fear* and *great joy*. Can you imagine what is going through their minds? *What if the disciples don't believe us? Jesus is alive! His body is gone! What if they think we're crazy? Why us? Wouldn't John and Peter be better choices to tell everyone what's happened?* They are fearful. But they are also joyful because they see what God is doing. They are seeing Jesus' kingdom moving forward and coming to life, and they are overjoyed.

Fear and joy. This is what it feels like to be called to be messengers and leaders. Fear and joy sometimes go hand in hand. Sometimes we're afraid of failure, of looking foolish, of coming up short. But we also have joy because we see what God can do and we see Jesus' kingdom moving forward. And there are few joys that compare to being trusted as a messenger in God's kingdom, partnering with him and being used by him to get his message to the world.

The problem arises when we think that the fear means we were never called in the first place. Fear is a natural part of the experience, but it doesn't disqualify the messengers. When we feel fearful as we step up in leadership, it doesn't negate the call. It means that God is stretching us beyond what we had perceived to be our limits.

MEETING JESUS ALONG THE WAY

Even though they are intimidated, the women obey the call and run to deliver the message. Their obedience honors Jesus. Matthew 28:9 says, "Suddenly Jesus met them and said, 'Greetings!' And they came to him, took hold of his feet, and worshiped him. Then Jesus said to them, 'Do not be afraid; go and tell my brothers to go to Galilee; there they will see me.'" As they proceed in obedience, Jesus meets them. And in the end the message goes out.

This is a tremendous promise for us. The self-doubt that we Asian American women feel is a problem only when we let it stop us from acting in obedience. When we step through our fears and take the risk, Jesus meets us in the very thing that he has called us to do.

I've experienced this time and time again. In leadership I continue to fight self-doubt. But the reason I keep coming back for more is that it doesn't end there. When I decide not to give in to my fears, when I do not quit, when I stop praying for God to strike me with the flu and instead focus on doing what God has called me to do, I meet Jesus. Or rather, he meets me. I see him come through and carry out his amazing work. Then I am grateful that the self-doubt didn't stop me from witnessing God's work. Ultimately, that's why I keep coming back.

The two Marys don't let hurdles or fear stop them from being obedient to God. They don't let self-doubt have the last word on what they will or won't do. Because they obey, they meet Jesus and see his message go forward. They move from self-doubt to empowerment. Perhaps they are our role models.

I wish I could say that the self-doubt has lessened each time I've been called to step up in leadership. But no. Sometimes when I am facing a big challenge, I still secretly pray for God to give me the flu. With each new step in leadership, the self-doubt comes up again because I am being entrusted with more and more.

But each time, I can look back and remember how Jesus was good last time and the time before and the time before that. And that is enough to remind me that, though I can see only fear and self-doubt on this side, Jesus is waiting to meet me on the other side. With each new risk, the memory bank of Jesus' faithfulness and goodness grows, so that I can say that Jesus has never let me down yet and he won't start now. Though the self-doubt still comes up, I see how God has healed me.

When I was leading a small group for the first time as a junior in college, I spent that year painfully battling all my insecurities. I constantly compared myself to other people and came up short. I thought, *I'm not funny like Alex or bold like Doug. I can't teach the Bible like Erin. I'm not good with people like*

Gia. I wondered if I had any gifts whatsoever and if God could use someone like me. I was pretty sure the answer was no.

Recently, I gave a presentation at a national conference. After I was done, an older leader said something I'd never heard before: "You are one of the most confident Asian American women I have ever seen." That surprised me! I quickly thought, *Well, if you only knew how insecure I feel sometimes . . .*

But then I began to see some of the imprints of God's healing and transformation. Years of listening to God and stepping through self-doubt to lead has brought God's grace and healing into my soul. I have grown from being that super-insecure junior. I am grateful for that. I'm learning more of how God has created me, and these days, instead of comparing myself to others, I am peaceful and increasingly content in how God has made me. I know more about how to focus on God and what he can do rather than on me and what I can't do.

When we say yes to letting God use us as messengers, we don't stay the same. He begins to transform us and to fill us with his boldness, strength and love. We don't have to live under a cloud of self-doubt.

STEPS TOWARD GROWTH

- First and foremost, God-centered leadership requires character. "Charisma is no substitute for character."[6] We need to let God speak to our fears and make us people of integrity and love.

- I would much rather have someone ask me to lead than to volunteer myself. We Asian American women are afraid to seem like we're putting ourselves forward. That's just not what you do. But we shouldn't always wait to be asked. It's important to take risks. Karis, a Chinese American lawyer, says, "I believe you can't wait to be 'discovered.' You have to seek God's mind and put yourself out there. I think these things are harder for Asian American women because we tend not to parade ourselves around. But if you ask me, it's better than being the one stuck organizing every potluck."

- The chance to lead on teams has helped me grow to love leadership. I've been on good teams and bad teams, but overall I love leading on or with a team. Many Asian American women enjoy working collaboratively, and this may be one of our special gifts. Leadership doesn't always mean taking a Lone Ranger approach. That's not necessarily what we see in Scripture, and the church and the business world are starting to seek more team-based leadership.

- If the theological issues regarding women's leadership are significant for you but you have never done your own study, it would be good to begin to examine them for yourself. At the end of the chapter you'll find some recommendations of books to start with. It was very helpful for me to learn the biblical basis of women in leadership. Once a man asked me why I led, and I was able to give a biblically based and articulate answer. He responded, "Wow, it's great that you have an answer that isn't just random."

- There will be times when you take risks in leadership, hoping to see God do something amazing, but instead it goes all wrong. You fail. Things don't turn out well. In those times, it is very tempting to give up. But I believe that God is more concerned with our faithfulness than with our apparent fruitfulness. In *The Making of a Leader,* Bobby Clinton reflects on God's purposes in the early phases of a Christian leader's development:

> God is primarily working in the leader (not through him or her). Though there may be fruitfulness in ministry, the major work is that which God is doing to and in the leader, not through him or her. Most emerging leaders don't recognize this. They evaluate productivity, activities, fruitfulness, etc. But God is quietly, often in unusual ways, trying to get the leader to see that one ministers out of what one is. God is concerned with what we are. We want to learn a thousand things because there is so much to learn and do. But He will teach us one thing, perhaps in a thousand ways: "I am forming Christ in you." It is this that will give power to your ministry.[7]

- Seek mentors. God-given mentors have helped me walk through every stage of growth so far. I am so grateful for them. They taught me about character and obedience to God, they encouraged me when I failed, they spoke truth into my self-doubt. They offered me the wisdom and perspective I needed. They challenged me. They taught me the Bible. They told me to try things I would have never dreamed possible. They believed in me. Seek out people like that.

Growth in leadership doesn't happen overnight. It's not just about what we do, it's about who we are and who we are becoming. Remember that God will finish what he started. "I am confident of this, that the one who began a good work among you will bring it to completion by the day of Jesus Christ" (Phil 1:6).

Happy and Free

Once some friends and I went to a beach at nighttime to have a bonfire and roast s'mores. That night was unusually warm. The guys in the group decided that they wanted to jump in the ocean and go for a swim. None of us had brought bathing suits or towels, but those minor details didn't matter—they wanted to jump in, clothes and all.

As they started to run down to the water, I really wanted to go too. Being in the ocean under the dark night sky sounded exciting. But I paused, looked around and saw that the other women in our group were sitting this one out, so I'd be the only woman in the surf. I hesitated and decided that I wouldn't go.

Already at the water's edge, one of the guys looked back and noticed my gaze. "Hey, aren't you going to come in too?" he called.

"I can't—I'm a girl."

"So what? Forget that, c'mon!"

I looked first at him and then at the waves crashing on the beach. *He's right. I should go.* Leaving behind my hesitations, I ran and dove into the water. Under the moon I floated, splashed by waves, in total freedom. I went home that night with mascara running down my face, wet clothes and hair made wild by salt water—feeling absolutely happy and free.

If you have ever felt the call of God to be a messenger and a leader but have said, "I can't—I'm a girl," God is like my friend, calling you to forget it and dive in to lead, happy and free.

Leadership?
I stand
Like she did, tall
Walking in her footsteps
The dust, the heat
The smell of wind and diesel

And my people followed

Epilogue
TRACEY GEE

May you know that your identity is triply blessed.
May you walk with a new name that God gives—
daughter, chosen, beloved—in place of shame.
May you know how to choose the better thing over all other things.
May you be free to fail, knowing that being loved
does not mean being perfect.
May you live in Jesus' power and presence in suffering.
May you experience God's forgiveness and redemption in your sexuality.
May you delight in being a woman.
May you grow into your own person
while learning to love and honor your parents.
May you thrive in friendships and relationships
that are healthy, whole and sources of life.
May you have a voice and be a voice for the
purposes of God and the voiceless.
May you lead with confidence.
May we experience all of what
God intended for us when he created us
as Asian American women.

I am about to do a new thing;
now it springs forth, do you not perceive it?
I will make a way in the wilderness
and rivers in the desert.
Isaiah 43:19

Acknowledgments

From all . . .

Thank you to the many women who lent us their stories of living in the tension of faith and culture and finding hope in Jesus. Thank you to our Daniel Project cohorts for your friendship and partnership. Thank you to Paul Tokunaga, who said, "I have a crazy idea! How about a book?" You have been a tremendous advocate and mentor in this process. Thanks for believing in us when we could hardly believe in ourselves. Thank you to Jeanette Yep for your sincere encouragement and lending us your expertise. We are grateful for you and all that you have contributed to this process—thanks, Auntie Jeanette! Thank you to Al Hsu, who has been a patient and fabulous editor. With wisdom, insight and grace, you have helped us walk through the unknown territory of writing a book.

Asifa

I'd like to thank my parents, Anwar and Jamila Din, who have embraced my calling as a full-time minister. I'd also like to thank my mentors, who have challenged me to use my voice through leadership. And a special thanks to Kim Porter, who has been a steadfast friend and partner in the gospel!

Christie

Thank you, Lord, for this book! This was a truly amazing process to be a part of, especially because of the leadership, friendship and hearts of each of the women involved. Thank you for letting me into the circle! My stories and experiences come from being a part of a one-of-a-kind family. Thank you Mom and Pop for raising me the best you could. These are our stories of trying, loving and growing. I'm proud to be your daughter! To my friends, Jeannie, Cheryl and Nikki, who edited, read and edited again. Thanks for your time and honesty. Thanks to supportive roomies, Sumer and Linda, who constantly prayed for me and the writing process. And to my husband, Brian—I love that you believe in me and support me in my crazy dreams. I'm grateful for your editing and ideas. You are truly a gift to me!

Kathy

Thank you . . . to the girlfriends who have so deeply influenced my life with Jesus and walked with me in the journey—Kathy Yang, Peggy Kim, Christine Pham, Jeanie Kim, Michelle Graham, Emily Fasick, Jennifer Greenberger and Regina Crosby. To the students and staff of InterVarsity at Northwestern University; they are living proof that my "work" is God's blessing. To my parents, Shin Woung Khang and Hea Chul Shin Khang, who continue to model lives of faith and faithfulness. To my amazing children, Bethany, Corban and Elias, who patiently waited for me as I finished one more paragraph and then, when I finally turned off the computer, greeted me with hugs, kisses and enough stories for another book. And to my husband, Peter Chang, who is my biggest cheerleader and toughest editor. He never complained, even when I was "in the zone" and unable to multitask. Even as deadlines pressed against difficult transitions at home, he prayed for me, encouraged me to dream, and served me tea during the late nights of writing and editing.

Nikki

Thank you Mom and Dad (Kasu and Fuzz) for journeying with me. Thank you Ba-chan, Ji-chan and Toyamas—you gave me my name and my history. Andrea McAleenan, your advocacy and sacrificial support helped this happen. Susi Jensen and Bobby Gross, thank you for contributing your professional opinion to strengthen the words of an amateur. To the draw group, Collin, Priscilla and Jason, thank you for your friendship, listening ears, challenging questions and stories. Thank you to the students and staff of

InterVarsity Christian Fellowship. Thank you Eastern leadership cohort and staff for teaching me on the journey. Thank you Lakeside and CLC Church for being family to me. And most of all, thank you Jesse for your partnership, care and fastidious editing. *In him we live and move and have our being* (Acts 17:28).

Tracey

Thank you to Peace Amadi and Lynn Kiang, my sisters and friends, who helped pray this book into existence. To all the students, staff and alumni of Bruin Christian Fellowship at UCLA and of Greater L.A.; you have been my community and I have loved learning to follow Jesus with you. Thank you to Evergreen Baptist Church of Los Angeles for being a wonderful church home. To my parents, Jin-Sheng and Teresa Shyr, and my sister, Alisa, thank you for your love and for all that you have invested in me. You are an amazing gift to me. And thank you to my husband, Benny, who is still my favorite person to talk to and laugh with at the end of every day. You were willing to tell me the honest truth that I needed a complete rewrite when I didn't want to hear it. Thanks for believing in me—you never doubted even from the very beginning. I love having you as my partner in the journey.

Recommended Reading

Asian Women United of California, ed. *Making Waves: An Anthology of Writings by and About Asian American Women.* Boston: Beacon, 1989.

Belleville, Linda. *Women Leaders and the Church: Three Crucial Questions.* Grand Rapids, Mich.: Baker, 2000.

Bilezikian, Gilbert. *Beyond Sex Roles: A Guide for the Study of Female Roles in the Bible.* 2nd ed. Grand Rapids, Mich.: Baker, 1995.

Blomberg, Craig L., and James R. Beck. *Two Views on Women in Ministry.* Grand Rapids, Mich.: Zondervan, 2001.

Chow, Claire S. *Leaving Deep Water: The Lives of Asian American Women at the Crossroads of Two Cultures.* New York: Dutton, 1998.

Fong, Ken. *Secure in God's Embrace: Living as the Father's Adopted Child.* Downers Grove, Ill.: InterVarsity Press, 2003.

Fong, Timothy P., and Larry Shinigawa, eds. *Asian Americans: Experiences and Perspectives.* Upper Saddle River, N.J.: Prentice-Hall, 2000.

Hamamoto, Darrell Y. *Monitored Peril: Asian Americans and the Politics of TV Representation.* Minneapolis: University of Minnesota Press, 1994.

Hesselbein, Frances. *Hesselbein on Leadership.* San Francisco: Jossey-Bass, 2002.

Hyun, Jane. *Breaking the Bamboo Ceiling: Career Strategies for Asians.* New York: HarperBusiness, 2005.

Keener, Craig S. *Paul, Women and Wives: Marriage and Women's Ministry in the Letters of Paul.* Peabody, Mass.: Hendrickson, 1992.

Lin, Tom. *Losing Face and Finding Grace: Twelve Bible Studies for Asian Americans.* Downers Grove, Ill.: InterVarsity Press, 1996.

McDonald, Skip. *And She Lived Happily Ever After: Finding Fulfillment as a*

Single Woman. Downers Grove, Ill.: InterVarsity Press, 2005.

Nam, Vickie, ed. *Yell-Oh Girls! Emerging Voices Explore Culture, Identity and Growing Up Asian American.* New York: Quill, 2000.

Newsom, Carol A., and Sharon H. Ringe, eds. *Women's Bible Commentary.* Louisville, Ky.: Westminster John Knox, 1998.

Takaki, Ronald. *Strangers from a Different Shore: A History of Asian Americans.* Boston: Little, Brown, 1998.

Tannen, Deborah. *You're Wearing That? Understanding Mothers and Daughters in Conversation.* New York: Random House, 2006.

Tatum, Beverly Daniel. *"Why Are All the Black Kids Sitting Together in the Cafeteria?" And Other Conversations About Race.* New York: BasicBooks, 1999.

Tokunaga, Paul. *Invitation to Lead: Guidance for Emerging Asian American Leaders.* Downers Grove, Ill.: InterVarsity Press, 2003.

Yep, Jeanette, et al. *Following Jesus Without Dishonoring Your Parents: Asian American Discipleship.* Downers Grove, Ill.: InterVarsity Press, 1998.

Zia, Helen. *Asian American Dreams: The Emergence of an American People.* New York: Farrar, Straus & Giroux, 2000.

Study Guide

QUESTIONS FOR PERSONAL REFLECTION
OR GROUP DISCUSSION

INTRODUCTION: ASIAN AMERICAN CHRISTIAN WOMEN

1. The author describes her experience in Thailand. Have you ever had a similar experience of seeing how women are mistreated in Asia? How did that affect you?

2. What is your ethnic background?

3. How do you think your gender and your ethnicity are connected? How do you feel about being a woman of your ethnic background?

4. What significant experiences have shaped how you understand gender and ethnicity?

5. Are you able to see yourself, an Asian American woman, as someone who God rejoices over?

CHAPTER 1: STICKS, STONES AND STEREOTYPES

1. What is your first memory of what it means to be Asian? (It might have been through a character in a movie or a book, or related to a statement someone made.) Describe what happened. Does it affect you today? In what ways?

2. What experiences have you had with stereotyping others or being stereotyped? How have you been stereotyped?

3. The author points to examples of stereotypes in the media. Can you think of other examples? How do they make you feel?

4. How do you understand the significance of names? How do you think God is renaming you or your community?

5. What do you hope the next generation will understand about what it means to be an Asian American woman?

CHAPTER 2: PULLED BY EXPECTATIONS

1. What are some of the expectations that you experience—spoken and unspoken—in your family and community? How did those get communicated to you?

2. Do you feel a tension between the expectations of Western and Asian cultures? How do you experience that?

3. Did you ever sense disappointment in your family because you were not a son? Did you ever feel less valued as a daughter? What does God want to say to that feeling?

4. Do you ever feel so pulled by the expectations of others that it's hard to know what you want or expect of yourself? Does it feel selfish to think of yourself?

5. How can you honor Jesus' desire for your relationship with him to come first? When have you been like Mary, sitting at his feet?

6. What does it mean "to choose the better thing"? How can you take steps to do that?

CHAPTER 3: PERFECTIONISTIC TENDENCIES

1. Do you struggle with procrastination or high expectations? The author links these to perfectionism. Do you agree or disagree?

2. Do you identify with the experience of being able to name the negative aspects of a situation but finding it hard to name the positive ones?

3. How do you feel when you make a mistake? What's your experience of making mistakes? How can you grow in finding freedom to fail?

4. Have you ever felt that God would love you only if you did things right?

What is the biblical truth? What is God's view of our flaws or sin?

5. Do you feel that your internal reality and external image match up? Why or why not?

CHAPTER 4: FROM SWALLOWING SUFFERING

1. How would you define suffering? What does suffering look like in the lives of those around you?

2. How have you seen people respond to suffering? How do you respond to your own suffering?

3. Do you think that suffering is abnormal and to be avoided? Or do you think that it is natural and inevitable? What helped shape your views?

4. Think of a time that you were going through pain. How did you handle it? How did you respond? Did you feel like you were swallowing suffering? If you are going through a hard time now, how can you take a step to interact with Jesus and be honest with him?

5. What do you learn about Jesus' character and compassion in his interaction with Mary and Martha?

6. Is God giving you an opportunity to come alongside a person who is suffering? How can you offer them God's comfort?

7. How does the promise of Revelation 7:15-17 increase your hope in the midst of suffering?

CHAPTER 5: FREEDOM IN SEXUALITY

1. What does it mean to be a woman? What do you think God's intention was for women? How did the Fall affect women?

2. Does sexuality feel like a good or scary thing to talk about? Why do you think that is?

3. What do Asian and Western cultures communicate about ideal feminine beauty? Do you feel pressure to conform to an ideal? How does that feel?

4. Do you often experience shame about your sexuality or about sexual experiences in your past? How is Jesus inviting you to experience his freedom and forgiveness? Have you ever talked about these things with someone else?

5. How can you celebrate with God when he says, "It's a girl!" with delight?

CHAPTER 6: DAUGHTER OF TWO WORLDS

1. What do you think of the concept of individuation? Do you think it is essential in the process of becoming an adult?

2. How do you feel the pull to be loyal to your family? When do you think you become an adult to your family?

3. Can you think of stories that your parents told of what it was like for them growing up?

4. The author says, "Good penmanship meant good parenting." How did your parents deal with your schoolwork?

5. How do you experience your mother's desire to tell you the truth? How do you experience your father's desire to dream for you?

6. What's your picture of a perfect parent? Where does that come from? How does it compare to your relationship with your parents?

7. How have you experienced God as a good and loving parent?

8. What are some characteristics that you appreciate about your parents? What is an area that challenges you as a child or parent in your relationship?

CHAPTER 7: FRIENDS OR ENEMIES?

1. Think about a couple of your friendships. How would you describe them? What are one or two things that you really appreciate about these friendships?

2. What blocks you from having strong and healthy friendships with other women?

3. Do you struggle with making comparisons with your friends? What does that look like for you? Where does it come from? How can you celebrate God's work in the life of a friend?

4. What do we learn from the example of Mary and Elizabeth's friendship?

5. What are some of the blessings of crosscultural friendships? What might be some of the challenges?

6. Are there aspects of your life that you hide from your friends? Ask God to help you to be honest in your friendships so you can be truly known.

7. What are a few steps you can take to deepen some of your friendships?

8. How would you describe your friendship with God? What are some specific ways that you would like to deepen your friendship with God?

CHAPTER 8: SINGLE ASIAN FEMALE SEEKING . . .

1. What assumptions or expectations do you have for romantic relationships? How can you hand those desires and hopes to God?

2. Are your hopes and expectations the same as or different from those of your family? In what ways?

3. What cultural expectations do you encounter from your family and community in your current life stage?

4. Does it feel tempting to believe that God is not good to you in the romantic realm? Why is that?

5. Are you in or would you consider a crosscultural romantic relationship? A relationship with an Asian man? What do you think the blessings and challenges of each would be?

6. What unique joys and challenges are you facing in the arena of romantic relationships?

7. How can you see Jesus' goodness in your current life stage? What biblical truth can you hold on to in this area of your life?

CHAPTER 9: GETTING USED TO THE SOUND OF MY VOICE

1. How did communication happen in your family?

2. What does it mean to "be a voice"? Do you think of yourself as a voice? Why or why not?

3. Do you feel you have a voice? What makes it difficult for you to use your voice? Is it circumstances, other people or internal blocks?

4. How are Esther, the woman with the alabaster jar and Phoebe role models for us? How do they demonstrate what it looks like to have a voice?

5. Are there nonverbal ways that you exercise your voice?

6. What things help you rediscover your voice? How can you use your voice to advocate on behalf of those without a voice?

CHAPTER 10: BECOMING LEADERS

1. Do you identify with the experience of self-doubt? What situations and circumstances come to mind? Where does this self-doubt come from? Do you think that having doubt cancels out being called by God?

2. Do you feel comfortable saying "I'm a leader"? Why or why not?

3. What are your theological convictions about women in leadership? What study have you done? What has been the most helpful to you in understanding this issue?

4. The author defines leadership as "having influence." Do you think of yourself as a leader? Why or why not?

5. What do you think of how Jesus interacted with women, and with the women in Matthew 20 in particular?

6. How have you experienced fear and joy in your opportunities to lead?

7. What distinctive contributions do Asian American Christians make to the practice of leadership?

8. What's a step you can take to grow as a leader?

Notes

Chapter 1: Sticks, Stones and Stereotypes

[1] Shelley P. Haley: http://college.hmco.com/history/readerscomp/women/html/wm_035405_sexualstereo.htm

[2] Timothy P. Fong and Larry Shinigawa, *Asian Americans: Experiences and Perspectives* (Englewood Cliffs, N.J.: Prentice-Hall, 2000), p. 264.

[3] Timothy P. Fong, *The Contemporary Asian American Experience* (Upper Saddle River, N.J.: Pearson, 2002), p. 192.

[4] Robert G. Lee, *Orientals* (Philadelphia: Temple University Press, 1999), p. 162.

[5] Jane Hyun, *Breaking the Bamboo Ceiling* (New York: HarperBusiness, 2005), p. 47.

[6] APAWLI, "Leadership Opportunities and Challenges: An Asian American and Pacific Islander Woman's Lens," typescript, p. 4.

[7] Interview, Veronica of New York.

[8] Interview, Jessica of Atlanta, Georgia.

Chapter 3: Perfectionistic Tendencies

[1] Richard Winter, *Perfecting Ourselves to Death: The Pursuit of Excellence and the Perils of Perfectionism* (Downers Grove, Ill.: InterVarsity Press, 2005), p. 27.

[2] Ibid., p. 43.

Chapter 4: From Swallowing Suffering

[1] Paul Tokunaga, *Invitation to Lead* (Downers Grove, Ill.: InterVarsity Press, 2003), p. 46.

[2] Debra K. Farrington, *Living Faith Day by Day* (New York: Perigee, 2000), pp. 40-41.

[3] Michael Wilcock, *Savior of the World* (Downers Grove, Ill.: InterVarsity Press, 1979), p. 103.

Chapter 5: Freedom in Sexuality

[1] Donald MacIntyre, "Base Instincts: Filipina and Russian Women Are Being Sold into Sexual Slavery in the Seedy Bars and Nightclubs That Serve U.S. Military Bases in South Korea," *Time Asia,* August 12, 2002.

[2] Mata Press Service, "Asia Hunts Sex Tourists," *The Asian Pacific Post,* September 7, 2005 <www.asianpacificpost.com>.

[3] "New Pregnancy Kit Makes Asia Jittery," *Asian Pacific Post,* August 11, 2005 <www.asianpacificpost.com>.

[4] Lisa Takeuchi Cullen, "Changing Faces," *Time Asia,* August 5, 2002.

[5]S. Allen Counter, "Whitening Skin Can Be Deadly," *Boston Globe,* December 16, 2003.

[6]Robbie Castleman, *True Love in a World of False Hope* (Downers Grove, Ill.: InterVarsity Press, 1996), p. 26.

Chapter 6: Daughter of Two Worlds
[1]Susan Cho Van Riesen, "Doctor or Lawyer?" in *Following Jesus Without Dishonoring Your Parents,* ed. Jeanette Yep et al. (Downers Grove, Ill.: InterVarsity Press, 1998), p. 59.

[2]Deborah Tannen, *You're Wearing That? Understanding Mothers and Daughters in Conversation* (New York: Random House, 2006), p. 39.

[3]Interview with Kathy, Chicago.

[4]Tim Clinton and Gary Sibcy, *Attachments* (Brentwood, Tenn.: Integrity, 2002), p. 31.

[5]Claire S. Chow, *Leaving Deep Water* (New York: Plume, 1998), p. 76.

[6]Kenneth Bailey, *The Cross and the Prodigal* (Downers Grove, Ill.: InterVarsity Press, 2005), p. 47.

[7]Paul Tokunaga, *Invitation to Lead* (Downers Grove, Ill.: InterVarsity Press, 2003), p. 40.

Chapter 7: Friends or Enemies?
[1]Amy Tan, *The Joy Luck Club* (New York: Putnam, 1989), p. 37.

[2]M. Robert Mulholland Jr., *The Deeper Journey* (Downers Grove, Ill.: InterVarsity Press, 2006), p. 23.

Chapter 8: Single Asian Female Seeking . . .
[1]Bill and Lynne Hybels, *Fit to Be Tied* (Grand Rapids: Zondervan, 1997), p. 141.

Chapter 9: Getting Used to the Sound of My Voice
[1]Amartya Sen, *Freedom as Development* (New York: Anchor, 1999), p. 231.

[2]Jane Hyun, *Breaking the Bamboo Ceiling* (New York: HarperBusiness, 2005), p. 5.

[3]Ibid.

[4]Sen, *Freedom as Development,* pp. 105-6.

[5]Lynette Clemetson, "Adopted in China, Seeking Identity in America," *New York Times,* March 23, 2006.

Chapter 10: Becoming Leaders
[1]Paul Tokunaga, *Invitation to Lead* (Downers Grove, Ill.: InterVarsity Press, 2003), p. 38.

[2]Ibid., p. 100.

[3]Walter Wright, *Relational Leadership* (Carlisle, U.K.: Paternoster, 2002), p. 2.

[4]Elizabeth Leung, "My Country Tis Not of Thee," in *Yell-Oh Girls! Emerging Voices Explore Culture, Identity, and Growing Up Asian American,* ed. Vickie Nam (New York: HarperCollins, 2001), p. 32.

[5]Tokunaga, *Invitation to Lead,* p. 102.

[6]Eddie Gibbs, *LeadershipNext* (Downers Grove, Ill.: InterVarsity Press, 2005), p. 128.

[7]J. Robert Clinton, *The Making of a Leader* (Colorado Springs: NavPress, 1988), p. 32.

About the Authors

The authors are all on staff with InterVarsity Christian Fellowship/USA, a national parachurch organization ministering to college students at over 500 colleges and universities in the United States. Each author was identified as an influential leader and invited to be in the Daniel Project, an executive leadership program designed to recognize and cultivate the leadership gifts of Asian American leaders within InterVarsity.

Nikki A. Toyama was born and raised in the Chicagoland area. After graduating from Stanford University she worked as an engineer in Silicon Valley. She then joined InterVarsity staff and served in campus ministry at

Stanford, University of San Francisco, and University of California at Berkeley. She now works for InterVarsity/USA and is based in San Francisco.

Nikki loves teaching Scripture and has spoken at training conferences in the San Francisco Bay area as well as at student and church conferences across the country. Nikki shared her journey at the Urbana 03 mission convention. She served on the executive leadership team for the Asian American Center (American Baptist Seminary of the West), designing conferences for Asian and Pacific Rim ministry leaders. She currently sits on the board of Mission Year and chairs a committee on multiethnicity advocacy. She is an M.A. candidate in organizational leadership at Eastern University.

Tracey Gee is a second-generation Chinese American who was born and raised in the Bay Area of northern California. After graduating from the University of California-Los Angeles, Tracey joined InterVarsity staff and served as the team leader of the undergraduate chapter at UCLA. She is an area director in southern California and has been integrally involved in leading, directing and speaking at Asian American student conferences.

Tracey also serves as the leader of the multiethnic resource team at Evergreen Baptist Church of Los Angeles in Rosemead, California. She is working toward an M.A. in global leadership at Fuller Theological Seminary. Tracey speaks and trains in the area of ethnic and racial development for students and campus ministry workers around the country. Her articles have been published in *Student Leadership Journal*. She and her husband, Benny Gee, are expecting their first child.

Kathy KyoungAh Khang was born in Seoul, South Korea. She is a graduate of Northwestern University's Medill School of Journalism. After graduation Kathy worked as a newspaper reporter at the *Green Bay Press-Gazette* and the *Milwaukee Journal-Sentinel*. She left journalism to join the staff of InterVarsity Christian Fellowship. Kathy serves as the area director at Northwestern University in Evanston, Illinois. She has participated in several national Asian American leadership forums. Kathy and her husband, Peter Chang, are honored to be the parents of three children, Bethany, Corban and Elias.

Christie Heller de Leon was born in Manila, Philippines, and emigrated to northern California with her family at ten months old. She graduated with a degree in sociology from the University of California at Berkeley, where she then served as an InterVarsity Christian Fellowship campus staff member for five years. While at Berkeley, she helped to pioneer the first InterVarsity ministry to Filipino students, called Kapwa, the Tagalog word for "shared identity" and "unity." Christie has taught at various conferences and seminars, including the Filipino-American Assemblies of God Convention of California, the Balikatan Conference for IVCF-Philippines alumni, and the Asian American Student Leadership Conference in San Diego, California.

Christie has also consulted with various northern California churches in their efforts to build collegiate ministries. As a teacher and trainer, she has passion for taking students into national and international urban contexts to learn about biblical and economic justice, poverty and evangelism. She lives in Davis, California, with her husband, Brian, and serves as team leader for the undergraduate InterVarsity chapter at the University of California at Davis.

Asifa Dean and her immediate family emigrated from Pakistan to southern California when she was six months old, and much of her extended family still lives in Pakistan where only 1 percent of the population is Christian. Asifa graduated with a B.A. in urban studies and education from the University of Redlands. After college, Asifa served as a campus staff worker and team leader with InterVarsity for seven years at Oregon State University. She moved back to southern California to be team leader at the University of California, Riverside.

Asifa serves on a national task force committed to the work of developing and training second-generation South Asian students. She also participated in the first North American South Asian Global Convention, held in Vancouver, British Columbia.